The NLP Professional
Create a More Professional, Effective and Successful NLP Business

In memory of my Dad, the most consummate
professional I have ever known and an
inspirational role model

The
NLP
Professional

Create a more professional, effective
and successful **NLP** business

Karen Moxom

First published in 2011 by

Ecademy Press

48 St Vincent Drive, St Albans, Herts, AL1 5SJ

info@ecademy-press.com

www.ecademy-press.com

Printed and Bound by TJ International, Padstow, Cornwall, UK

Designed by Michael Inns

Artwork by Karen Gladwell

ISBN 978-1-907722-55-4

Contents

Definition

*NLP pro·fes·sion·al/*prəˈfeSHənl ~

A practitioner* of NLP, who is serious about their business
and who wants to make a difference by delivering their NLP
services in a responsible, congruent and ethical way.

---

*practitioner in this sense is anyone who holds an NLP qualification,
from Diploma to Master Trainer.

Acknowledgements

I have many people to thank, who have all supported me in my life and in my role as an NLP Professional:

To all the ANLP staff, Associates, International Ambassadors and Volunteers, without whom there would be no Association for NLP.

To all the people mentioned in this book, and all NLP Professionals, especially members of ANLP, who are out there, making a difference every day.

To those who gave us this gift called NLP, Richard Bandler and John Grinder, and the ANLP Fellows – Steve Andreas, Judith DeLozier, Robert Dilts, Charles Faulkner, Stephen Gilligan, Christina Hall, L Michael Hall, Tad James, Bill O'Hanlon, Julie Silverthorn, and Wyatt Woodsmall.

To all the NLP Professionals I have had the privilege to meet and work with, including Michael Carroll, Joe and Melody Cheal, Dee Clayton, Jane Douglas, Sharon Eden, Nick Kemp, Jeremy Lazarus, Judith Lowe, Tony Nutley, John Seymour, David Shephard, Robert Smith, Emily and Roger Terry, Paul Tosey, Sally Vanson and Lisa Wake. Many of these trainers generously give their time, knowledge and understanding to be there for me and ANLP and I am truly grateful for their support.

To Pauline Newman and Kathy Strong, who first introduced me to NLP and unknowingly gave me the signposts for what continues to be an amazing journey.

To Mindy Gibbins-Klein and Ecademy Press, for believing in me and encouraging me to publish this book; to Sarah Abel, who is the most professional and thorough editor I have ever worked with.

Acknowledgements

To Shirley Cully and Suzanne Henwood, whom I met on my own NLP training many years ago and who have been close and supportive friends ever since.

Most importantly, to my two boys, Tom and Daniel, for their unwavering faith and patience, which enables me to be both a mum and a Professional.

Foreword

I remember as a young man going for an interview and being asked 'What comes to mind when you think of the word "professional"?' I was taken aback by the question and mumbled some trite answer. The truth was, I had never thought about it. I wish I had read Karen Moxom's *The NLP Professional* before that interview. Not because I knew anything about NLP back then, but because it would have helped me understand what it means to be professional. While this book is aimed at the NLP practitioner, much of it could apply to being professional in any field.

The word 'professional' derives from the Latin, *profiteri*, meaning 'to declare publicly'. Being professional means recognising what we publicly say and do reflects on who we are. Furthermore, as practitioners of NLP our behaviour reflects on the whole field. In terms of Robert Dilts' Logical Levels model, the lower levels (Environment, Behaviour and Capability) represent the higher levels (Beliefs and Values, Identity and Larger System). In some quarters NLP is at best mocked and at worst held in contempt. If enough people follow the guidance in this book we can support the efforts of the growing numbers attempting to change those perceptions and make NLP a recognised, credible and respected subject.

I make a distinction between '*a* professional' – a role – and '*being* professional' – a process. If Carl Rogers, one of the granddaddies of the human potential movement, had decided to write a book on this subject I guess he would have called it *On Becoming Professional*. We don't become professional by getting a certificate. 'Becoming' is an ongoing and developmental process that never completes. We are always en route.

The NLP Professional contains lots of practical tips on how to set up and run a professional business, but for me the heart of the book is how Karen breaks down the complex process of becoming professional into seven easy-to-understand themes.

Karen says that integrity and trust are the two most important values that guide professionalism.

Integrity has two meanings: being honest and acting from moral principles; it also means whole and coherent. Integrity is not something we can have in one sphere of our life and not another, it's not something we can do some of the time. In my experience, integrity needs to be demonstrated consistently because opportunities to cut corners, over-sell, be 'economical with the truth', manipulate, turn a blind eye, etc. are ever present.

The other important value, *trust,* has a counterpart – *trustworthy*. Being professional means being worthy of trust. Over the last twenty years, many of my clients have said they want to trust more; never has a client said they want to be more trustworthy. Now why is that? I suspect a 'cognitive bias' is involved. My guess is that like many other 'self-serving biases' most people would consider themselves above average when it comes to trustworthiness – which of course is statistically impossible. Tellingly, when people hear about self-serving bias they often smile and remark that they know others who have that problem!

There are two ways to counter such a bias, and both of them depend on recognising that we *might* have a bias and not know it. We can either honestly re-evaluate our own behaviour and intentions (in 12-Step Programmes this is known as 'a searching and fearless moral inventory of ourselves'); or we can seek feedback from people we admire. I recommend doing both. What we *do* with the information is what counts – not just in the short-term flush of feeling free, but in the months, years and decades that follow.

If we combine integrity and trustworthiness we get the *impeccability* that Carlos Castaneda acquired from the teachings of shaman don Juan Matus. Being professional means delivering quality service and performance – even when we are not at our best, or the situation is not making it easy. Finding a way to be as prepared as we can and then giving our best, whatever the circumstance, is a hallmark of professionalism.

By establishing ANLP International as a community interest company with its multitude of services, magazines and journals, and by writing this book, Karen is not only demonstrating her professional credentials, she is helping others to do the same.

James Lawley
London
July 2011

A personal message from
David Shephard,
President of the American Board of NLP

Karen Moxom's *The NLP Professional* is a vitally important contribution to the future of the field of Neuro Linguistic Programming (NLP).

You may be wondering what qualifies me to make such a claim.

I was first introduced to NLP in 1990 by reading Anthony Robbins' book *Unlimited Power*. I very quickly decided it was something I wanted to pursue as a career path. I was certified as a Trainer of NLP in 1994 and a Master Trainer in 1996. I have been running my own NLP Training Institute since 1993 and have certified in excess of 1000 NLP Trainers around the World. I am on the Advisory Committee of ANLP International here in the UK and I'm the President of the American Board of NLP.

In 1990 there were only four NLP Training Institutes in the UK. Now there are over 100 to choose from. Over the last twenty-one years I have seen NLP Trainers come and go and as part of my responsibilities for the ANLP and ABNLP I have to deal with customer complaints. Fortunately, very rarely do I hear a complaint about the standard of training; unfortunately it's the professionalism and business ethics of the trainer that are in question.

Just like any field that is enjoying phenomenal growth there are 'rogues' or 'get rich quick merchants'. Whether that be practitioners and trainers making false or exaggerated claims, saying they are qualified when not, not sticking to guarantees and promises or standards and guidelines. This has got to such a point that I recently heard an NLP Trainer at a conference say, 'There's nothing particularly special about me. I'm just very good at stealing other peoples' material and saying it's mine'. He got rapturous applause! Unfortunately there are people in the NLP world who consider this modelling!

In *The NLP Professional*, Karen addresses all of these issues and more. She gives us a road map to stand out from the crowd for our professionalism, as well as skills. For the continued development of NLP and for the peace of mind of the consumer this is vital. Without it NLP has a questionable future. Each of us in the NLP field has the responsibility to follow Karen's lead and demonstrate professional behaviour in our NLP businesses whether that is as a practitioner, coach or trainer.

David Shephard

Certified Master Trainer of Neuro Linguistic Programming
President of the American Board of NLP
July 2011

Introduction

▼ *Do you ever meet opposition and scepticism when you mention NLP?*

▼ *Do you worry that your considerable investment in your training may go to waste?*

▼ *Are you ever concerned NLP may be a fad or a trend, and may fade away in favour of new ideas or more established ones such as cognitive behavioural therapy (CBT)?*

▼ *Do you want to create a more professional, effective and successful NLP business?*

If you answered 'yes' to any of these questions, then these may be the reasons you have picked up this book.

'The difference that makes a difference'...it is one of the first things we learn to look for when we are taught about modelling excellence. Discovering this can make the difference between 'good' and 'great', 'pass' and 'distinction' or even 'success' and 'more feedback' (because as we know, there is no failure, only feedback).

NLP can often be the difference which does make the difference. NLP can be the catalyst which alters someone's perception enough for them to make the changes they desire.

So as NLP practitioners, we are catalysts for change, and this means we can have a positive social impact on society. The challenge can be although we know we can do this, NLP is still not always recognised as a credible and viable option.

NLP continues to evolve and is now at a crossroads and we, as NLP practitioners, do hold its future in our hands. We collectively have the choice to raise our game, and take those next steps towards getting NLP universally recognised as a credible and complementary option. There are other options and sometimes, it does seem easier to do nothing and let things run their natural course...and this is a choice.

So, what exactly constitutes a 'Professional'? There are two definitions of professional[1] we would aspire to meet as NLP Professionals:

> 1. *A person competent or skilled in a particular activity.*
>
> 2. *A person engaged in a specified activity as a main paid occupation rather than as a pastime.*

The NLP Professional is about considering the field of NLP as a professional one. It is about making connections between your actions as a practitioner of NLP, and considering how these could possibly impact upon your business and the professional field of NLP, which is still in its infancy.

The NLP Professional is about looking at NLP from a different perspective – it is about chunking up and considering NLP as a field of practice; applying perceptual positions and some of the useful tools and techniques we have learned to the field of NLP, and collectively accepting responsibility for taking NLP to the next level.

This book will question some of the current practices in our field, and challenge whether these are ultimately useful if our desired outcome is to raise the profile of NLP and create a profession which has credibility, respect and recognition, and can stand proudly alongside other helping professions.

---

[1] Oxford Online Dictionary, www.oxforddictionaries.com.

My desired outcome from writing this book is that you will have a professional, effective and successful NLP business. Ultimately, the more success you have as an NLP Professional, the more people will benefit from the positive applications of NLP and society will eventually take a few positive steps forward.

I want you to be proud of being an NLP Professional and be happy to stand up and be recognised for the NLP skills you offer and the empowering changes you can make to the lives of others.

I will offer you some practical steps to take so you can develop a more professional, effective and successful NLP business. I will offer you some ideas and perspectives which may help you to reflect upon the part we all have to play in ensuring a bright future for the field of NLP, because ultimately, the success of NLP leads to your success as an NLP Professional.

When you read this book, you will have some different perspectives and reframes to use to develop your practice as an NLP Professional, you will have a greater understanding on how to take action to raise the awareness of NLP, and you will understand the impact you have on creating a positive and successful future for NLP, which ultimately has a positive impact on your NLP business.

If, as you are reading this book, you come across any unfamiliar NLP terms or phrases, please do refer to Robert Dilts and Judith DeLozier's NLP Encyclopedia for further information.[2]

After all, ultimately, we are all part of the difference that makes a difference and so we can influence how the field of NLP develops.

So, what qualifies me to write *The NLP Professional*?

I have been leading the Association for NLP (ANLP) since 2005 and I do, therefore, have a slightly different perspective on the field of NLP. At ANLP, our role is twofold – to represent

---

the views of our members and also to provide information and knowledge to the public about NLP, which means we talk to both NLP professionals and the public on a daily basis, and often act as the bridge between the two.

Sometimes, I think we are the 'empowering connections facilitators', and our aim is to create an environment which increases the possibility of linking people who have a need with people who have a solution (in this case, NLP).

I am passionate about NLP and I strongly believe NLP is one of those personal development philosophies which really can have a positive impact and therefore can make a difference...to an individual, to a team and to society as a whole.

And because of where NLP currently sits in society – embraced by a few, ridiculed by others and unheard of by the majority, I believe one of the things we can do to change this is to work together. Indeed, we believe working together will play a key role in ensuring NLP has a strong and positive future.

My first encounter with NLP was when I did a five week 'Introductory course in Neuro-Linguistic-Programming' at Barnet College. At the time, I had no idea what 'Neuro-Linguistic-Programming' was, but I thought it was either something to do with personal development, something to do with computer programming...or both. As I had an interest in both subjects, and it was only a five week course, I had nothing to lose by signing up.

It is said you can pinpoint those times in your life which are turning points, and discovering NLP at an evening class in Barnet was definitely one of mine. I had always been interested in personal development, had read my fair share of books and attended workshops...and found however good my intentions whilst I was immersed in the subject, I seemed to forget all about these wonderful self development tools I had learned about once I was back in the real world.

NLP was different. There is something uniquely empowering about NLP which has stayed with me and really did enable me to make lasting, sustainable changes to my life. In fact, one of the main reasons I chose to follow up my introductory course with a Practitioner course was somebody had mentioned 'NLP was one of the few things which had made a lasting difference to their life'. If this was going to be the case, then it seemed like a good investment at the time.

I was sceptical. My background includes a scientific degree and a 20 year career as a management accountant...could something as simple as altering the appearance of an image in my head by changing the sub modalities REALLY make THAT much difference to the way I handled a particularly challenging person in my life? It could, it did, and it still does...and has resulted in a more positive, healthy and sustainable relationship with this particular individual.

Before I took over the Association I spent my days enabling small businesses to take more responsibility for their accounts and develop a greater awareness of their financial situation. By doing this, they were able to make more informed decisions, more quickly and more successfully. I was using my own NLP skills daily to improve the effectiveness of my one to one training, as well as doing some additional coaching alongside this.

In 2005 I was approached by my former NLP trainer and asked if I was still pursuing my dream – the one I had shared some years earlier when I was the demo subject on my own Practitioner training. My dream had been to create a centre where like minded people could congregate and share ideas, and work together to support each other, so they were empowered to make an even bigger difference in society using NLP and coaching.

I had been pursuing my dream in my spare time, but from a completely different angle, and so when I was offered the opportunity to take over ANLP, I paid off the debts of the Association, and found myself the proud owner of a one page website, the ANLP domain name, a magazine which had all but ceased production and a membership list.

I do realise now what a controversial decision I had made and now, I am really glad I made this decision. Early on, there were many times when I really did feel like I had bitten off more than I could chew and what carried me through those tough times was my belief NLP is an empowering and potentially life changing philosophy which can make a positive difference to the lives of others.

Furthermore I believe if there could be 500 or 5,000 or even 50,000 NLP Practitioners making a difference because of the support they have from ANLP, then together, we would be making a far bigger difference to society than I could ever hope to achieve on my own.

So since 2005, I have worked really hard to build ANLP into the strong, independent and impartial social enterprise which it is today. In 2009, we were awarded the title Small Business of the Year by Hertfordshire Business Awards and I was honoured to receive the award for Hertfordshire Woman of the Year.

You may be wondering what continues to drive me, and spur me into taking action – why is it so important to me NLP becomes accepted as a credible, professional solution to some of the challenges life can throw at us?

The answer is simple – I want NLP to become more widely recognised so it will be embraced by the education system, and as a result children will be given a greater opportunity to benefit from NLP, reach their full potential and will be set up for success in the future.

I have watched both my children struggle with the education system for different reasons and I am driven by our experiences and the attitude of many educational establishments I come into contact with.

If NLP was a more credible, acceptable and widely recognised solution in society, then Local Authorities would recognise the impact of NLP, schools would be able to adopt a more balanced approach, enabling children to achieve their full potential and be set up for success – rather than the current system which appears to be driven by data, targets and academic achievement and favours those children who can more easily conform to the system.

Whilst this may not be your reason for wanting NLP to become more credible and widely accepted in society, I am betting there is some reason aligned with helping others which brought you into NLP in the first place. So I am guessing you too, have your own reasons for wanting NLP to be a more credible and widely accepted option for people seeking solutions to their challenges.

Finally, I do just want to reassure you this book is not about standardising NLP, and making it so process driven the flair and flexibility is lost – it is more about how we can work within the parameters of existing society whilst maintaining the flexibility which drives NLP to continually evolve and create an mindset where we can have both creativity and professionalism in the field of NLP.

CHAPTER ONE

Adopting a Professional Attitude

> 'By the time I was 22, I was a
> professional. A young and flawed
> professional, but not an amateur.'
>
> Stephen Sondheim, composer (1930–)

Why would you want to adopt a professional attitude in your line of work…and what exactly is a professional attitude?

Too many practitioners of NLP never consider the impact of their attitude on their business. It doesn't always occur to them their own appearance and the way they present themselves (personally and professionally) may influence the number of clients they have or the level of fees they can charge.

NLP Professionals understand if you want people to pay good money for your services, you need to look, sound and feel like you are worth the investment on every level. To borrow a well used phrase, 'your attitude determines your altitude'. So in order to encourage people to part with their money for your services, it is important for you to have a professional attitude.

Attitude is something which NLP practitioners find easy to adopt. Even if we are not yet engaged in NLP as our main paid occupation rather than a pastime we can act 'as if' we are. People are more likely to engage with us if we are acting in a professional way, because this gives them confidence in our ability.

Being a professional means outwardly demonstrating you have the skills and ability to meet the needs of your potential clients. If you are serious about your NLP business, then I would strongly encourage you to treat it like a profession and behave like a Professional.

NLP is partly about fun and learning in a relaxed and enjoyable environment...and if you want to make a career out of your NLP, then there are some elements of this game you do need to take seriously. Remember, it is possible to have a professional attitude, run a successful business and enjoy yourself, and I know many NLP Trainers who do successfully combine all three elements.

It is all very well stating a professional attitude is necessary, but what constitutes a professional attitude and how could you go about achieving a more professional approach to your business?

Creating well formed outcomes... the business plan

As NLP practitioners, we already know all the benefits of creating some well formed outcomes and having some SMART goals defined, and maybe, sometimes, we forget to apply these things to our own business. One of the things I learned is there is always a good time to make a business plan, however long your business has been running.

All professionals know the value of a business plan and all effective businesses have a plan. This plan can be a written record defining where we want our business to go and how we intend to achieve these plans, broken down into smaller, more manageable steps – I know, this sounds familiar to you already.

Schools are a prime example of having a good working model from which they operate. On top of the layers of existing policies and procedures they have, all schools have an annual

School Improvement Plan (SIP), which specifically outlines what goals they wish to achieve in the coming year, how they will achieve these, who is responsible for ensuring they are achieved and key timed deadlines for achieving various steps along the way.

This is a great model for success and maybe we could take some of these planning models and apply them to our own business.

My friend and her husband recently returned from a round the world trip, which was similarly planned with great precision. It could have been perceived as a huge amount of planning for a big holiday – although wouldn't it have been a huge disappointment to them if the highlight of their trip had been to visit Ayers Rock, and they had ended up missing out because they had run out of time, money or both, due to ineffective planning?

Like every good plan, there does need to be some flexibility. One NLP Coach I know, Tim Gunning has two rules for planning.

1. *There should always be a plan.*
2. *Nothing ever goes according to plan.*

I use these rules simply to remind myself a certain amount of flexibility is required when running a small business.

So even though, as a small business, you may require a great deal of flexibility, having a business plan really can make a difference. I know it is partly thanks to our business plans and well formed outcomes, we were ultimately rewarded by winning two awards at the Hertfordshire Business Awards in 2009.

TIP

Google 'business plan' to find some useful templates, which will provide you with a starting point for creating your own plan.

I view our business plan a bit like embarking on a water ride or flume at the swimming pool. Our plan is the course we take so we can get from the top of the water ride to the bottom (which usually involves arriving in a pool of water with a big splash). Along the way, we may veer off course slightly and slip from side to side as we rush down the water slides, and yet the sides keep us on course enough to reach our destination – landing with a big splash at the end of the journey…and we've had some fun along the way.

There are some times when it is really obvious to have a plan and we would never set out without one. We had the honour and privilege of being able to build our own house in 2007… and we would never have even started if we hadn't had a set of plans from which to build.

Yet even with a set of plans, we did have to adapt, deviate slightly and make changes along the way – the foundations had to be deeper in one area because we discovered, once we started digging, the ground structure varied from one end of the plot to the other; we changed the internal layout dramatically before we started building, and then made further alterations along the way, once we saw the rooms actually taking shape; the kitchen layout probably changed at least 20 times before we ordered the units; the whole plan, from start to finish, became one big project which in hindsight, utilised so many of the NLP strategies we all know and understand…and I'm pretty sure we tested all the presuppositions of NLP along the way…

…*the map is not the territory (and neither were the room sizes once we actually laid them out);*

… *there is no failure, only feedback (how many times did we lay out little paper cut-outs of kitchen units before we had a layout we were all happy with?);*

… *we all have the resources we need (especially at midnight, when we just needed a bit more energy to finish painting the kitchen before we went to bed);*

… respect for another person's model of the world (it's very important to remember this when dealing with council planning departments and conservation officers);

… one cannot not communicate (except with plumbers who fail to turn up on site…and even then, there are ways).

The benefits of having a plan could be the difference that makes a difference for your business. Certainly, as far as the house was concerned, having a plan was the one thing which drove us on to completing the project because we were all very clear, as a family, about what we were aiming for and we were constantly able to remind ourselves of the ultimate goal (and living in a caravan on site may have helped with the motivation as well).

I'm sure we have all experienced times in the past when we have set out to do something without having any real plan – we'll go with the flow, see where this takes us…and this works really well if we don't have a specific outcome or intention.

I love going out on a Sunday afternoon and just driving somewhere – heading north (or south, east or west), turning left (or right), taking this narrow lane and having the curiosity to see where we end up and what treasures we may discover along the way (usually a tea room, garden centre, or a simply discovering a stunning view). On the other hand, if I have to be in a particular place at a certain time for a meeting, then my journey is planned – out comes the sat nav, in goes the destination and I'm off.

As far as our own effective business goes, having a plan has been our sat nav and has been the difference that makes a difference because we all know what steps we need to take in order to get us a bit closer to our goals. The plan sometimes just acts as a reminder for us because we know exactly what we need to be doing; and at other times it really does help us to focus and stay on track by guiding us to the next step and reminding us of the bigger picture – the outcome and the reasons for doing what we are doing.

Maintaining a balance

Whilst we may need to use our business plan on occasions to remind ourselves of the bigger picture and the path towards our ultimate outcomes, it is also important to remember to maintain a balance between 'working in' and 'working on' our business.

In case you need to be reminded, 'working in' our business is often what we do best, it's where our area of expertise lies and it's why we chose to set up our own business in the first place. If you trained as a coach or NLP practitioner, then when you are working 'in' your business you are working with clients, coaching them or running training courses. When you are working 'on' your business, you are working on all other aspects of your business – marketing, administration, planning, continual professional development (CPD), i.e. all those other aspects of your business which don't directly earn you any money, but which do form a necessary part of the whole business.

I had an accounts client who had a good balance between working in and on their business. The directors had an eye on the management of the business at the same time as actually contributing to the profitability of the business by being out on part time, but lucrative contracts themselves.

On occasions, this balance would waver, when there was a greater demand for contract work and a project was nearing completion, or when the contract work dried up a bit and they could then spend more time planning and structuring their business, and overall, they maintained a balance between the two.

Too much of one or the other can have a detrimental effect on the business. Another client discovered this when their contract work dried up completely for a while, after a period of intense work and pressure. They had been working so hard in their business, they had taken their eye off the bigger picture, i.e. future contracts, and suddenly found themselves with no planned work.

At this point, they panicked, and ended up making some rash short term decisions including selling their house, simply because they found themselves quickly moving from a position where they had loads of money coming in, to one where they had very little money coming in.

This same fluctuating cycle can happen with NLP practitioners, who have periods of being really busy with clients with hardly any time to work on the other aspects of their business. After all, when demand is there and client contact hours are very high, the natural tendency is to take all the work offered, just in case. But then, as a skilled NLP Professional, when those clients have all reached their goals, achieved their outcomes and moved on, there follows a quiet period. This often happens because you are so busy working with the clients, you may not have time to do your marketing.

Ideally, it would be great to maintain the balance so even during the busy periods, the marketing wheels are still turning so there is always a steady trickle of new business coming in.

One way to achieve this balance is to schedule in time to work 'on' your business as well as 'in' your business – treat marketing, sales, social media and business development activities as if they were another paying client and schedule them into your diary.

Another thing you can do is decide on your ideal role within your business and work towards this – do you want to be the hands on coach because you enjoy working with the clients and helping them? If so, this is what you ultimately need to aim for, with most of your time being allocated to clients and employing other people to support you whilst you are working in your business, e.g. a marketer, administrator and/or bookkeeper.

TIP

Set up your business in departments, even if you don't have enough staff to manage each department . . . yet. We have done this ourselves and find it is much easier for us to manage the business and more clearly define where our most pressing needs are, especially in terms of potentially buying in or delegating services.

This could be when we sometimes come up against the age old paradox of balancing time with quality and finances – at some stage, every successful business has dealt with the delicate balancing act between providing high quality goods or services, when measured against the time it takes to provide these services and the cost of doing so.

In larger organisations, people are employed to undertake both aspects of the job in order to keep the organisation running smoothly. A nurse mainly works in the business of caring for patients, i.e. they spend the majority of their day having direct contact with their patients and focusing on them. The matron of the ward, on the other hand, will spend the majority of their day working on the business of running a ward, managing the nursing and auxiliary staff, the processes and the policies and have far less direct patient contact. And the hospital administrators, ideally, ensure the books are balanced and the money is available for both nurse and matron to fulfil their roles.

Even then, it is still vitally important to have the right balance of personnel throughout the organisation – there are times when we frequently hear about poor services in the NHS, because there were too many administrators and bean counters and not enough nurses and doctors to actually care for the patients. So even in large organisations, there do seem to be a few challenges balancing service provision with the budgets.

Thankfully, we tend to run smaller businesses than the NHS, and so we have the flexibility to introduce more creative solutions than those employed by the NHS. So what creative solutions could you find to ensure you maintain a balance between working in and working on your business? These solutions will differ widely from person to person and the flexibility comes in utilising whatever works for you and your particular business.

TIP

You probably already have an idea of your financial value in terms of what you charge for your services (by the hour or day). Remember to use your own value when deciding which aspects of your business you could delegate – if your charge out rate is £50 per hour, and a bookkeeper will charge you £20 per hour for dealing with your invoicing and accounts, then where is your time best spent – invoicing or seeing another client?

We have several members who have started using a virtual PA, because this frees them up from doing those tedious administrative jobs they do not enjoy, and allows them to spend time on the more lucrative aspects of their business. One of them particularly values the work of their administrator because of the freedom this gives her and the opportunities which arise as a result of having some of those administrative tasks taken off her own plate.

A businessman I knew on the other hand, views the world very differently. He only employs salesmen and all staff are expected to focus on how much money they can bring in every month and how much they can contribute to the bottom line. This would work in a large company, where there are other departments to support the sales team, but doesn't seem to work in his small business, because everyone has to work 'in' the business and there is nobody taking care of any of the other tasks which form part of any successful business, such as administration, marketing and advertising.

Our member who employs the virtual PA is steadily growing her business because she has managed to even out some of the wave by effectively sharing her workload. She seems to be more calm and relaxed, and is very happy to delegate certain tasks to ensure they get done and the business stays on an even keel.

The businessman's business, on the other hand, seems to be more of a roller coaster ride for everyone involved, which could be fun, I guess, and is probably more stressful (this is my personal opinion, based on the number of bailiffs who used to turn up looking for payment because nobody has had time to settle any bills).

So yes, there is a balance to be found between working in and working on your business, especially if you do want to have an effective one.

TIP

Establish exactly what services you would like to delegate to a virtual PA, and how you want to use their services – would you be happy working completely virtually, i.e. no face to face contact, would you prefer some direct contact via the occasional meeting, or would you prefer to work with someone coming to you on a regular, or irregular basis, i.e. more freelance administrator rather than virtual services.

The benefit of procedures and paperwork

You are possibly thinking as a former accountant, I am obviously a very procedural person in terms of Meta Programs (or Language and Behaviour (LAB) profile). I had better confess now I actually have a heavily options Meta Program, *and* I perceive the value of procedures to be huge because they are a great way to save time and increase efficiency...which enables me to spend far more time doing the things I enjoy doing.

Even as an accountant, I would run through the procedural bit (processing the invoices, balancing the bank account) quickly and easily with the minimum of fuss and effort, so I could then get to the bits I enjoyed – the problem solving bits; the trouble shooting; empowering others by creating some simple processes for them to follow, so their accounts would take them two hours a month rather than two hours a day.

In hindsight, once I had learned about NLP, I realised a lot of what I was doing with my clients was developing a model for them, a strategy which would work well for their business and which was broken down enough for them to be able to replicate it – does this sound familiar?

Michael Gerber encourages procedures and policies in his amazing book, *The E-Myth Revisited*.[1] By having processes in place, we are able to delegate tasks to others, whilst still maintaining our sense of what our business is about – the essence of our business. As soon as we have a detailed model for the way our business works, it is very easy for someone else to pick up and complete these tasks on your behalf.

I have only recently read *The E-Myth Revisited*, and my initial reaction was to wish I had read it years ago, because I could have saved myself a lot of time and energy. I do believe, though, we come across things when we most need them, and when we are open and ready to receive the wisdom, so maybe it was the right time.

So, you can ensure you are running an effective business by having some effective paperwork and processes in place. I'm not talking about NLP processes here, I'm talking about business processes, procedures and policies which you, or anyone you employ, can follow and which will enhance your business efficiency and professionalism.

These processes, procedures and paperwork can be as simple as having a particular strategy for handling a new client. This

---

[1] Gerber, M.E. *The E-Myth Revisited: why most small businesses don't work and what to do about it.* New York; HarperCollins, 2001.

way, whether you are the person who has the initial contact with your potential client, or it is your virtual PA, your receptionist or your assistant, there is a method, style and strategy for dealing with them. Your efficiency and organisation can have the knock on effect of demonstrating your professionalism and potentially increasing the confidence your client will have in you.

How does paperwork come into this? In two ways:

1. *Externally improving communications.*

Imagine what impression your business card has on someone, when it is the first thing which someone sees relating to you (especially nowadays, with business cards being left in the reception areas of health clubs and paraded in special card holder displays in the lobby of various stores).

Your business card may also be the only reminder someone takes away with them after a business networking meeting, or at an exhibition or conference. It may even be your card is passed on to another potential client by someone who thinks they may be interested in your services. So you would like your business card to be an informative reminder for your potential client.

I went to a great workshop recently, entitled 'PR for Virgins'. The presenter asked for a group of people to give him their business cards. He then shuffled them all up, and spread them out in a fan shape like a deck of cards, and presented them back to his audience…and because he was holding them upright, just like a set of cards, all we could see was the back of the cards.

He then asked the original group to pick out their own business card – and anyone who had a plain white back to their card had no idea which card was theirs. The PR message was you have two sides of a business card, so use both of them to enhance your communication with others.

2. *Internally improving business efficiency.*

By having special ways of dealing with people, and having policies and strategies in place to cover different potential scenarios, you have more chance of appearing confident, competent and professional in the eyes of your potential client.

If you have clear, up to date client records and efficient ways of keeping track of your clients, potential clients and ex-clients, you and your colleagues can always handle any calls and queries, because you have clear and simple processes for handling enquiries.

Contrast this with a national institution helpline – I had to call them three times recently because I needed to know how to update some details with them...each time I called their helpline, I was given different advice, and the reason I had to call them three times was because the first two pieces of advice didn't work.

One could have assumed they have a clearly laid out process for changing details, so my query could have been handled efficiently and quickly...unfortunately, unlike most other small businesses, they do not need to work on winning and retaining customers as we all have to deal with them anyway.

As a small business, you do need to work on winning and retaining clients, so having systems in place to help you manage your potential and current clients will help.

TIP

There are many customer relationship management (CRM) systems on the market, so just Google 'CRM systems' to come up with a multitude of web based or software systems – you will find at least one to suit your particular requirements.

Another good reason for having an effective set of policies, procedures and paperwork in place is to protect both you and your client. This paperwork can include some basic client information forms, and various checks to ensure you have assessed the appropriateness of taking on this new client as well as a contract to ensure you have some clear boundaries and agreements in place.

I have come across various incidences where having these strategies in place have protected both the client and the NLP practitioner. Whilst delivering a Practitioner training, NLP Trainer, Tony Nutley, was increasingly concerned about the way a particular student was behaving on his course. Eventually, he felt obliged to ask the student to leave because he was increasingly concerned about the effect this student was having on the other students, on the trainers and their assistants.

Tony was able to handle the scenario successfully because he had clear boundaries already in place through a contract and pre-screening forms; he also had policies for recording various observations and incidents and had documented these throughout the course. These procedures benefitted the students because it meant both successful and unsuccessful students could receive powerful feedback, and every student had a file documenting their progress throughout the course. Tony also benefitted because in the unlikely event something could go wrong, he had the backup of his paperwork as documented evidence.

Nowadays, with the chances of potential litigation increasing, having procedures and policies in place is something which insurance companies could become more insistent upon. In fact, I understand one of the insurance companies which currently covers NLP practitioners will only support a claim if seven years of client notes have been kept by the NLP practitioner...so make sure you read the small print, because they too have policies in place to protect them in the event of a claim.

Presenting yourself as a Professional

Having worked with small and medium businesses for the last 20 years, I have found one of the most important things to take into consideration is to look, sound and feel like a professional on every level. We already know about the VAK representational systems (visual, auditory and kinaesthetic) and we know how much visual appearance/body language can affect first impressions.

It does vary considerably from person to person, so perhaps, something we can choose to model is best practice we have seen in other practitioners. One of the things I learned as a management accountant was looking, sounding and feeling like a professional did not necessarily mean wearing a black suit all the time – it is very much about adapting to your surroundings.

A few years ago I visited the bank with the managing director of a successful media business, who was one of my clients. I was his management accountant and we were going to the bank to ask for a £1 million loan to acquire another company. I turned up to the meeting looking every inch the professional management accountant – black suit, smart shoes, briefcase and reams of supporting paperwork, all professionally produced and neatly filed in a presentation folder. My client turned up wearing a black T shirt and jeans, and a blazer. I was horrified, because at the time, my model of the world equated professional with a black suit (and there was no flexibility in this model).

I watched my client closely during the presentation (only years later did I appreciate I was actually running a quick modelling project) and I realised between us, we were presenting a completely professional package. My client may have looked unprofessional in my eyes, but he was very appropriately dressed for a managing director of a media business, and what's more, he spoke passionately, he knew his business model inside out, his demeanour oozed confidence...and his resources, i.e. his documents, his business cards and presentation folders (and his accountant) were all professionally presented and top quality...and yes, we got the loan.

As I have alluded to in this example, professionalism is not just about your personal appearance. It is about every aspect of you which is available in the public domain. So think about what quality and professional look, sound and feel like to you, because this initial impression, as you know, counts for a lot.

TIP

There are a few useful websites for Professionals including **www.companieshouse.gov.uk** *for information on company structures;* **www.hmrc.gov.uk** *for advice on all aspects of UK taxation, VAT and employers' obligations;* **www.ipo.gov.uk** *for information about protecting your own intellectual property.*

There are many things you may wish to convey to your potential clients and somewhere down the line, I'm pretty sure confidence is going to be one of them – your client will want to feel confident you are the one they can work with; they will want to be confident you have the capability to support them through change; they will want to be confident they are making the right decision.

Part of this confidence will be conveyed to them by how you present yourself and your business. I don't know about you, but I would certainly have more confidence in a dentist who has clean and tidy looking premises, a smiling receptionist with gleaming teeth and the obligatory fish tank in the waiting room...as long as the fish are clean and shiny, like my teeth will be when I'm done.

It is so simple nowadays for anyone to Google you and get your online profile in an instant – so what do these potential links say about you? Do you have the right balance of professional messages and social messages on the internet? If you were to Google your name right now, what would you come up with? Do you have a presence in those professional arenas where you would like to be conducting business?

From a marketing perspective, remember people buy people and certainly in the NLP profession, you are selling your services as an NLP Professional to your potential clients. How do you want people to feel when they have come into contact with you? This is an important aspect of your business because there are emotions involved here – NLP is all about subjective experience. The image you present to the public is the image your potential clients will walk away with.

Are you presenting the image you want to convey to the world (or at least your potential clients)? Think about the tools you use to promote yourself – your business cards, your website, your social media activity, your promotional leaflets. Do they convey the messages you want them to?

For example, how do you deal with phone calls and other auditory means of communication – do you have a dedicated business line at home (so you can convey a professional image rather than have the family picking up your calls)? Do you have an answerphone to pick up messages when you are busy with clients? Do you pay for an answering service to pick up calls in your absence? Or do you rely on your child/partner/dog to entertain your clients until you can get to the phone.

Research indicates 70% of people do not leave a message on an answerphone, so could this have an impact on your business? We have frequently received feedback suggesting people are relieved when they get to talk to a person and, sometimes, their buying decision will be influenced simply by the fact we answered the phone and they were able to talk to us in person.

TIP

Consider using an answering service to manage your calls – there are many around offering a flexible wide-ranging service. We recommend a variety of business resources on our website,
www.anlp.org/business-resources-for-nlp-professionals.

One of the other important things for you to consider, as an NLP Professional, is the location of your business. You have far more flexibility in this respect than some businesses because you are primarily selling your services. If you were opening a retail outlet, for example, it is usually a good idea to have either a physical presence somewhere where your customers can visit you, or a great web presence where customers can find you and buy online.

So, do you work from home, work from office premises, or find another solution? Again, there are pros and cons associated with each option.

If you are thinking of working from home, there are some obvious benefits in terms of cost, proximity and convenience. Basing yourself at home is ideal in many respects, and do make sure you take everything into consideration. Where do you want to see your clients? Is there a separate part of your home you can dedicate as a client area? If not, what could a client experience when they come to visit you? Is this the best impression you want to create for them and does this work for them? What is the potential impact on the rest of the family and how does working from home affect your house insurance? Is it a safe enough environment from which to run a one to one business?

A friend of mine actually attended her Master Practitioner training at the trainer's home and said afterwards this was one of the most distracting aspects of the course. It certainly gave her some important practice in honing her senses (to block out the sound of the washing machine) and state management.

Other trainers, who have a more professional attitude, do run successful trainings from their home on a regular basis, because they have modelled the attributes of a professional establishment.

Many practitioners can base themselves at home because they then travel to clients' premises or hire an appropriate workspace when required. Obviously a trainer can hire training rooms for running an NLP training, and it is also possible to hire consulting rooms by the hour or take a reasonably priced room on a part time basis within one of the many alternative practitioner or holistic treatment centres.

I do know of practitioners who work in hotel lobbies and reception areas, and certainly in London, some hotels are getting wise to this and starting to make charges for occupying the space. There are many creative solutions to be found when considering the best location for your business.

TIP

Many centres now offer room rates by the hour – consider hiring one of these, especially when a hotel lobby may not be the best environment to conduct a meeting. See recommended resources on our website,
www.anlp.org/business-resources-for-nlp-professionals.

Summary

I have covered some of the basics about adopting a more professional attitude, and what contributes to the perception of professionalism.

Once you are able to encourage more people to part with their hard earned cash, your NLP business will grow. If more NLP professionals were to adopt a more professional attitude to their business, then NLP as a whole would become recognised more easily as a profession. And if NLP was more easily recognised as a profession, alongside doctor and lawyers and accountants, then demand for your services would increase and you would be able to charge a higher amount for your services.

So you are already playing a significant part in the field of NLP and we do all have a share in taking responsibility for NLP becoming more widely established as a profession, with some beneficial knock on effects for everyone in NLP.

CHAPTER TWO

Being Congruent with What You Do

> *'I challenge you to make your life a masterpiece.*
> *I challenge you to join the ranks of those people*
> *who live what they teach, who walk their talk.'*
>
> **Tony Robbins, motivational speaker (1960–)**

Authenticity is detectable – you don't have to be NLP qualified to work out whether someone is being congruent (i.e. their values and beliefs match their actions). If a practitioner of NLP is advocating their client could use NLP to improve their relationship, or further their career, or overcome their fears, or be a better parent, then they need to be walking the talk and demonstrating they are a living breathing example of the positive powers of NLP.

NLP Professionals understand how important it is to be a great ambassador for their business and recognise by demonstrating the impact of NLP on their own life, they are the best piece of evidence they have to demonstrate NLP works.

NLP Professionals understand NLP is about attitude, it is about communication and it is, in a way, a philosophy for life...you know you need to make sure you are in the category of people who walk their talk, rather than 'doing as I say, not as I do'.

I think I grew up in a world of clichés – among the many I learned as a child was 'practice what you preach', and this is something which has stayed with me over the years.

NLP is about subjective experience, so it does make sense we need to experience NLP ourselves before we can expect others to do the same. A lot of NLP is also content free, so even though it is important we experience the practice of NLP, we will all apply this to our own unique issues and challenges, and the results will probably be unique to us.

NLP is about practice and although there are theories which underpin it, it tends to work best when you take action and do it. As Carl Jung said, 'children are educated by what the grown-up is and not by his talk'.

Being authentic

If we have experienced NLP for ourselves, in whatever context, we are able to approach our clients from a place of understanding. We do need to have experienced the six step reframe, anchoring, sub-modalities, perceptual positions and parts integration for ourselves, regardless of the actual content, so we are better placed to act as a guide for our clients to do the same.

I wonder if you have ever received one of those emails, promising to teach you the techniques you need to become a millionaire, simply by attending their amazing wealth course.

It seems quite often, the people running these courses are not actually millionaires themselves...but they do know of someone who has made millions following their strategies. So they are hoping you will take a huge leap of faith and accept their offer to teach you some techniques which they themselves have not successfully put into practice...yet.

I listen to many personal development CDs, and in my opinion, one of the best sets I have ever listened to, was recorded by Gill Fielding, the wealth expert and millionaire.[1] She knows about creating wealth and it was very apparent,

---

[1] Fielding, G. and Thomson, P., 'My daughter wanted a pet, so I bought her a greyhound'.

from the CDs she had experienced poverty as a child, but has become successful and really is a millionaire now.

She is walking her talk and sharing her experiences with others and there is something about her which is real and believable. She has a genuine desire to share her knowledge and guide others along the path she has already travelled.

In this particular instance, I think context and content of the experience are very important and relevant to what was being offered. However, as an NLP practitioner, it is the experience of having used NLP ourselves which is important, so we are genuinely walking our talk and only asking our clients to do things we have been prepared to do ourselves.

Sometimes the content can be important, and could end up forming the niche business we can then offer as a service to others. NLP trainer, Neil Almond, really has used his NLP to good effect in very extreme personal circumstances. Neil and his partner Andy were travelling in Australia in 2008, when their small plane crashed. Yes, they really did crash, into the sea, and they all survived. Neil and Andy have probably utilised every NLP skill they could muster in the following 12 months to help them overcome this trauma.

What I find most incredible and admirable, is Neil and Andy flew back to Australia 12 months later, despite their understandable fears and trepidation. Neil has shared his experiences with us and they were serialised in our magazine, *Rapport*. Neil does now have a specific niche for applying his NLP and he really can claim to be an expert in overcoming flying phobia.

I'm not suggesting we all need to fully experience the context in which we apply our NLP – this would be a bit extreme, especially if it involves any sort of danger. As we know, everyone would have had a different type of experience, even in those extreme circumstances.

What I am suggesting is in order to fully engage with your client, there does need to be a level of congruence within you which comes from being in a place of understanding. If you are congruent with and believe in what you are doing, your client stands a much better chance of achieving their own outcomes.

If you are asking a client to take a leap of faith and work with you utilising NLP skills and techniques to overcome their challenge, then some real experience of NLP and some understanding of what they are going through to overcome their challenges could help. This is why all NLP courses do need to have a large element of experiential learning and why NLP just cannot be learned simply by reading a book or completing an online training course.

Sometimes we can be unconsciously incongruent within ourselves. I say unconsciously because we may not be aware of this incongruence at the time. You will probably be familiar with Robert Dilts's Logical Levels and how he links environment, behaviours, capabilities, beliefs, values and identity.

Incongruence can arise when there is inner conflict between our own logical levels. Our beliefs can play havoc with our own congruence, especially those beliefs around capabilities.

I remember experiencing this inner conflict when I attended my initial coaching training weekend. We had an inspiring talk on the Sunday afternoon about how to get clients. We were encouraged to take action as soon as possible and start recruiting clients as soon as we got back home, if not before. One of the potential sources for new clients was through networking groups, and we were tasked with joining one of these groups as soon as possible.

I duly searched the internet on Monday morning and found my most local networking group, which met in the golf club at 7 a.m. every Thursday. They had a spare slot for a coach and were delighted to welcome me as a new member.

The inspirational talk I had heard the previous Sunday managed to motivate me until 6.59 a.m. on Thursday morning. The moment I walked into the golf club and was introduced to a suitably suited businessman, I felt completely at home as a management accountant...and completely out of my depth as a coach.

I had 15 years experience as a management accountant and trainer, but I had only been coaching for one weekend, and hadn't yet finished reading the coaching manual. Yet there I was, answering questions about coaching...and standing up giving a one minute presentation about what I did for a living, as a coach.

There is acting 'as if' and yes, I can do this, yet I felt, in this particular situation, what I was doing was completely wrong. At the time, I had no experience as a coach apart from one weekend of coaching like minded people who were attending the same course. I felt very uncomfortable and I was terrified of actually winning some business as a coach.

In hindsight, I realise my lack of confidence and my incongruence must have been shining through like some sort of warning beacon, clear for all to see, despite my best attempts to act 'as if'. Acting as if only works for me if I believe in what I am doing and have some sort of congruence between my beliefs and my competence.

TIP

Make sure you do have congruence within yourself and your own beliefs do align with your business, so you can deliver your business messages with authenticity.

I know this now because I can compare this experience with one which had happened a few years previously and, with hindsight, I have been able to work out the difference that made the difference.

When I was on the parents' committee of Tom's school, four mums (including myself) had the brilliant idea of raising money for the Meningitis Trust. We wanted to do this because the young daughter of one mum had had meningitis a few months early. She had, thankfully, fully recovered, but it had been an anxious time for all of us.

Right from the start we had the motivation, the drive and the belief we could do this. Our aim was to raise £10,000 for the Meningitis Trust in one day by running one big event.

Nobody believed we could do it; they said we were overstretching ourselves and our goal was impossible. Even the local Round Table only raised between £6,000 and £7,000 a year at their annual summer fair, and this was an established event being run by a well known and well respected local fundraising group. What chance did we possibly have to beat this?

Yet we believed we could do it, and we spent six months acting 'as if' we were running a major event to raise funds for charity. We believed in our cause and we spent hours on the phone and in meetings, talking to local, national and international companies and asking for their support.

On 1 May 1994, we held our event, a fun run and fair, and we raised £13,000 in one day for the Meningitis Trust. We achieved and exceeded our goal because we were all very congruent with what we were doing and our beliefs were fully aligned with our actions.

Saying one thing and then doing another does send out mixed and confusing messages. And yet, as we know, confusion does seem to lead to a greater understanding because, quite often, the confusing messages allow us to realise there is some sort of incongruence, or set of double standards going on.

I continue to be amazed (or perhaps amused?) when I visit a health care establishment, like a hospital, and see health care workers standing outside the main entrance smoking. Even worse is when the patients are out there as well (they can be identified as the ones wearing the regulation hospital gowns). Whatever one's beliefs about the rights and wrongs of smoking, I think most people understand it is bad for one's health…so what sort of mixed message do we get from this scenario?

Whilst there are some elements of NLP which we would use for specific reasons to deal with particular challenges, there are other elements of NLP we can bring into our own lives, every day, including:

▼ *Values and beliefs.*

▼ *The presuppositions of NLP.*

▼ *Building rapport.*

▼ *Checking ecology.*

▼ *Applying perceptual positions.*

▼ *Being 'at cause'.*

Values and beliefs

I believe two of the most important values held by NLP Professionals are integrity and trust.

When you start working with a potential client, you are entering into a partnership and relationship with this client. In my map of the world, integrity and trust are essential to any successful partnership.

Essentially, in a coaching or NLP partnership, we are holding the space for the client to make the changes they want. By holding the space I mean we are giving our clients a safe environment and space (metaphorically and sometimes literally) to be able to explore new possibilities and make changes to their own lives. It is about cause and effect, and us giving them the space to be at cause and take responsibility for themselves, and take the action they deem necessary to get the results.

It's a bit like when our children do their homework. I sit with my younger son on homework nights and effectively hold the space for him, so he can focus on taking the right action to complete the required homework. For a child with special needs, this kind of focus can be quite challenging, and it is so tempting sometimes, simply to give him the answers and do his homework for him. However, 95% of the time, I do manage to hold the space for him and allow him to find the answers for himself...even if it does take an hour longer.

You may have experienced this special and safe environment when you were doing your own NLP training. When I was doing my NLP training, I was lucky enough to find myself with some great people and we were all able to create and hold the space for each other. We were all going through some pretty deep changes ourselves, and there had to be a great deal of trust and integrity between us so we could successfully take those steps for ourselves and deal with our own challenges.

Sometimes, a client does need to have enough trust in you so they can develop the confidence they need to take the required action. Quite often, all it needs is a bit of courage, and to have someone like you, holding the space and creating the safe environment for them to take the step, is what makes the difference.

I remember first getting into the driving seat of a car, ready to learn to drive. My driving instructor talked to me first, explaining exactly what I needed to do, where the safety net was (the dual controls) and in hindsight, I realise what they were doing was building some trust and rapport with me before I set off (in fact, they probably needed to trust me as much as I needed to trust them).

I remember doing all the necessary checks, turning the key and starting the engine, taking the handbrake off, performing mirror, signal, manoeuvre...and then putting my foot on the accelerator for the very first time. The car lurched forward and we gave a very good impression of a kangaroo for the first five minutes or so (I was very relieved we had no audience).

Once I had made those first tentative moves, I then had the confidence to do more, and by the end of the first lesson, thanks to the nurturing and patience of my instructor, I was on my way to becoming a driver.

Many years later, I experienced a whole new level of trust when I took my son Tom and his friend on holiday. We had the opportunity to do some abseiling from a tower, across the lake to an island...and then swing back into the lake before being lowered into a boat and brought back to shore...easy, especially for someone who is not so keen on heights.

The children, it seemed, were oozing confidence and were keen to give this a go. I played the supportive mum role and took them over to the tower, ready to shout words of encouragement as they abseiled into the distance. I had spent the morning building up their enthusiasm and excitement in readiness for the highlight of the holiday.

When we reached the tower, which had seemed quite small from a distance, everything suddenly seemed a whole lot bigger and more daunting. Tom turned to me and said, 'you go first'. This hadn't been part of my plan at all, but I found myself at the top of the tower, being strapped into various harnesses and safety equipment and standing on the edge of a very tall platform, looking out over the lake.

Tom and his friend were standing at the bottom of the tower, shouting words of encouragement up at me...and reminding me about positive mental attitude and the benefits of trying something new (wasn't I supposed to be saying this to them?). They trusted me to walk my own talk and in turn, I found myself putting a huge amount of trust into the complete stranger who was harnessing me to this very thin rope which stretched for miles into the distance.

I stood on the edge of the platform for what seemed like ages. The instructor murmured words of encouragement and ran through the safety checks one more time. I put every ounce of faith and trust into him and the safety equipment and I stepped off the platform...and enjoyed moments of complete exhilaration and excitement greater than I have ever experienced before. More importantly, I had done it, I had walked my talk and my son and his friend, who had put their trust in me, were now prepared to have a go themselves.

TIP

Be prepared to pace and lead your potential clients before they are ready to engage your services (or even those of another NLP Professional). You may know the benefits of what you can do for them, and they may need convincing.

If we are to be completely congruent with what we do and present an air of authenticity, then we do need to have our values and beliefs aligned with what we actually do.

I had an accounts client whose strap line was 'people first, profit a close second'. I really liked this strap line as it aligned with my own values and I felt this was a company I could work well with and support to reach their financial goals.

What I started to realise, over time, was this strap line was just a set of words, strung together to form a nice phrase. The values which were reflected in the strap line were not reflected in the actions of the company or its directors. To be more accurate, what the strap line should have said was '*Certain* people first, profit a close second'. As their management accountant, I was in a better position than most to realise this.

I did hold on to the client for a good few years after realising this, but again, because of the mismatch with my own values, I felt my own authenticity was being compromised. The day I left the company, I felt like a huge weight had been lifted from my shoulders (even if I was financially poorer as a result).

TIP

If you are feeling uncomfortable working with a particular client, check your values and see if there is a potential mismatch. Sometimes, no matter how much you know you can help someone, if the values don't match, it can play havoc with a business relationship.

The Presuppositions of NLP

The Presuppositions of NLP[2] form part of the philosophical thinking behind NLP. The presuppositions are designed to give us some useful insights into behaviour and therefore give us greater understanding, and perhaps more tolerance of others.

So once we have an awareness of the presuppositions of NLP, we can apply these to our own lives. If we have embraced NLP in our lives, as well as encouraging others to do the same, then the presuppositions come as part of the package. They are part of the richness which is NLP and underpin it in so many ways.

It took me a while to understand the philosophy behind presuppositions of NLP, because I started off by thinking they would only work if everyone in society adopted them. I now realise when I adopt the presuppositions of NLP, my life is easier because they can add meaning and give a useful reframe to explain the behaviour of another person.

A few years ago we experienced an interesting situation at the Vitality show. We had taken a stand at the Vitality show to promote *Rapport*. Spending three days at an exhibition can be very demanding, so it was a case of all hands on deck, and help had been recruited from all available sources, including my partner who was more than willing to come along and do his bit, even though he didn't know a great deal about NLP.

He was manning the stand and handing out copies of *Rapport*, when a person approached him and asked if *Rapport* was anything to do with ANLP.

---

[2] See Appendix.

'Yes', he replied, 'Do you know about NLP?'

'Yes, I used to be a member of ANLP.'

'Well, ANLP is up and running again, you should visit their website to find out more.'

'"Should?"' they snapped back, '"Should"…you obviously know nothing about NLP'….and they walked away.

My partner was mortified and really concerned he had made some terrible mistake and really upset this person in some way. Actually, I believe the opposite is true:

This person, who clearly did know something about NLP, could have applied their knowledge of the presuppositions of NLP to the situation and walked their own talk. They could have known enough to have respect for another person's model of the world; could have known enough about the communication model to understand the effect of their own behaviour; could have understood we were 'using the resources available to us at the time'; and could have recognised whilst there is 'no failure only feedback', it is possible to find more appropriate ways of delivering the feedback. To this day, I still wonder how, exactly, this particular 'behaviour had a positive intention', although I successfully reframed it as 'they were just having a bad day'.

TIP *Remember there is no failure, only feedback. One of the most valuable ways you can improve your own business is by accepting feedback as free consultancy advice and being grateful for the opportunity to make positive changes.*

Building rapport

In the above example it could be argued rapport had not been built strongly enough at the beginning of the conversation, so everything went downhill from there.

It is easier to build rapport with someone when you are genuinely interested in what they have to say, and you do have some empathy with them. Aren't you more likely to engage with a client if you can unconsciously build rapport with them?

Generally, people are much more aware nowadays of building rapport. Once upon a time, the telephone salesman would simply ask to speak to the managing director, make some comment about the weather and then launch into their spiel about their product or service.

Now, they spend the time attempting to build rapport first, and go through all the rapport building questions... 'and how are you today?', 'what are you doing?', 'how could this be made easier for you?'...and this is how we can help. Great salesmen have learned to do this naturally and will engage with you and identify your requirements before they sell you their solution.

Sometimes, though, you can tell these salesmen are just going through the motions. They have been told what they need to do and how to do it, and sometimes they are just doing their job and consciously attempting to build rapport. If we are aware of this, it could have the opposite effect, i.e. put us off, rather than encouraging us to buy.

I remember being in an interview with someone who clearly had some understanding of rapport and was keen to demonstrate their skills by consciously trying to build rapport with me. Throughout the interview, I was matched and mirrored to within an inch of my life, my every action was copied and I confess after an hour of this, I was exhausted. I had become so self conscious of my own actions I completely lost the flow of my own thoughts and I felt less able to effectively communicate. Funnily enough, this particular relationship did not go any further.

Genuine rapport works wonders – we know it does and it will make a difference to the results you get with your clients.

NLP allows us to understand how rapport can work and be used effectively…as long as we are walking our talk and slip in to doing it naturally.

Checking ecology

We could make our own lives a lot easier sometimes, by taking a step back to think and plan before we act. We learn about checking ecology on our NLP course, i.e. considering the impact of our intended actions on our existing lifestyle and relationships, and yet sometimes, we do get so caught up in the moment we may lose focus, both on our intended outcome and our own ecology.

NLP trainer and entrepreneur, Emma Sargent, wrote a very honest and open piece for *Rapport*, where she admitted her move from London to the West Country had not exactly gone to plan because they simply hadn't considered all the potential consequences of making such a move. For a while, although life was idyllic, their business really suffered and they had to find far more creative ways to rebuild their business in another part of the UK.

We once received a complaint about an NLP practitioner from a woman whose boyfriend had undertaken a one to one NLP consultation. Neither of us had any idea what the original consultation was about, but the result was the boyfriend had packed his bags and left this woman. She wanted to complain about the NLP Practitioner on the basis she was not happy with the results of her (now ex-) boyfriend's consultation and felt NLP was to blame.

We had to help her manage her state and expectations and support her in determining some more realistic outcomes. We have no idea whether this was the intended outcome of the consultation, although it was a timely reminder about the importance of recognising the potential consequences which may result from taking action...whether or not NLP is the catalyst.

Checking ecology applies equally to your clients and to your own business, and it is important to recognise any potential knock on effects, or consequences when building an ecologically sound professional NLP business.

Applying perceptual positions

Perceptual positions is a valuable NLP tool which has a variety of powerful uses when working with clients. As an NLP Professional, you certainly do not need me to go into the detail of using perceptual positions effectively with clients.

There are many areas where an NLP Professional can also benefit by applying the concept of perceptual positions to their own business. This can be an invaluable way to evaluate aspects of your own business in a more detached and rational way, and review your business from another perspective.

TIP

Use perceptual positions for evaluating your own professionalism and hone in on various aspects of your business.

For example:

▼ *What impression do you want clients to get when they look at your online profile?*

▼ *What impression do potential clients get when they look at your online profile, and is this the same as the impression you want to convey?*

▼ *What would your trusted mentor advise in this situation, so the message you wish to convey via your online profile is the message your clients actually see when they view your profile?*

Being 'at cause'

It is important for NLP Professionals to recognise the value of being at cause and acting with responsibility. As an NLP Professional you have been hired to do a job, and this job is usually to support a client in metaphorically moving from where they are now to where they want to be.

The client must take responsibility for making those changes and take the action which will move them from A to B, because, ultimately, it is their life and their choice. But as the professional, it is your responsibility to correctly assess the situation and decide on the appropriateness of your actions and interventions, strategies and models you may choose to introduce to your client.

I had a client who employed me as their management accountant because their previous businesses had failed, due to a variety of reasons including 'rubbish bookkeeper, bad debts, staffing issues.' You name it, their business had suffered from it and all these things had resulted in their previous two businesses going into liquidation.

I did their accounts for a while, and because I kept the accounts accurately, it quickly became apparent the business owner was actually the main drain on the business, because he was continually borrowing the business funds for personal use which was effecting cashflow...even though I took responsibility and demonstrated this to him, it was not something he was prepared to accept.

Our businesses can be affected by the recession, the lack of clients, others not taking responsibility for promoting NLP widely enough . . . but at the end of the day, if every one of us takes 100% responsibility for running our own business effectively, we stand a much better chance of succeeding.

Summary

Applying the philosophies, tools, techniques and strategies we learn in NLP to ourselves and our own business can be very relevant. Walking our own talk will lead to us, as NLP Professionals practicing with a greater degree of congruence and authenticity.

By being a great ambassador for your business, you are also acting as a great ambassador for NLP, and raising awareness around NLP and the positive influence it can have on life.

Be congruent with what you do

CHAPTER THREE

Demonstrating Best Practice

*'I do the very best I know how –
the very best I can; and I mean to keep
on doing so until the end.'*

Abraham Lincoln, American president (1809–1865)

This is the one area many practitioners of NLP shy away from – demonstrating best practice. Many practitioners of NLP feel their creativity could be stifled, and others just want to standardise what NLP has to offer. Some practitioners of NLP simply do not understand what best practice is and have no idea how easy it is to adopt best practice principles for themselves.

NLP Professionals embrace the opportunity to demonstrate best practice, because it allows them to demonstrate they have an awareness of their responsibility to their clients. Best practice allows you, as a Professional, to accept accountability for your actions and very much puts you at cause with your clients.

In turn, this gives reassurance to your potential clients you are taking responsibility for your actions and your part in the process of change – not only is this setting a great example to your clients, it also gives them reassurance NLP could just be a credible solution to their particular issue.

When considering best practice for NLP Professionals, there are various models we could adapt and adopt from other professions, including:

▼ *Scope of practice.*

▼ *Ethics in practice.*

▼ *Adopting minimum standards of practice.*

▼ *Realistic representation of NLP as a solution.*

▼ *Referral systems.*

▼ *Coaching, mentoring and supervision.*

Scope of practice

As a practitioner, it is so important to be aware of your scope of practice, i.e. know what you are capable of handling in a professional situation. However well qualified and experienced a practitioner is, they may not have the right experience to deal with every issue which arises.

When I received my certificate to prove I was an NLP Practitioner, I was excited I had qualified. Everything I had been working towards came together when I received my NLP Practitioner certificate...and then I stepped out into the real world. What, exactly, did this qualification mean? What, specifically, was I qualified to do?

To be honest, when I received my NLP Practitioner certificate, I felt qualified to manage my own life much better than I could some months earlier. In hindsight, I now understand this particular training was designed with this purpose in mind, so I did come out with what I expected, as did everyone else on my course. We all knew and understood we had been enlightened and educated in some really useful strategies for managing our own lives.

The thought of putting 'NLP Practitioner' on my business card briefly crossed my mind, and was instantly dismissed again – I had attended a fairly short course in NLP, and my initial outcome for attending the course had been achieved. I had, however, discovered along the way NLP was immensely powerful and really was making a difference to my life in a way no other personal development training course had done.

I personally did not want to put NLP Practitioner on my business card because I did not feel I was in any way qualified to practice my NLP on other people and advertise I was doing so. As I became more unconsciously competent and more confident, I did find I was using my NLP to enhance my work as a management accountant and accounts trainer.

One of the questions we are asked by newly qualified practitioners is: 'Am I a therapist now?'

The short answer is no, probably not.

I was very aware receiving my NLP Practitioner certificate did not qualify me as a therapist of any sort. Given the dictionary definition of a therapist is 'a person who treats physical, mental or social disorders or disease', and the definition of a practitioner is 'a person who practises a profession or art', there are very few NLP qualifications which will automatically qualify you as a therapist.

NLP and coaching differ from therapy because they start with a belief the client is OK, well and whole, and simply wants some help moving from where they are now to where they would like to be. Therapy can be more about delving into the past and analysing the smallest things in great detail, unpicking them so it is possible to understand the impact of past experiences.

As part of this journey, it may be NLP will be used to alter one's view of past events and reframe them in some way so they become more manageable and have less effect on current behaviours, but NLP can be content free, whereas therapists do include references to the specific content.

Another reframe is to look upon therapy and NLP coaching as being presented with a packet of sunflower seeds and a garden which looks ready for planting. NLP and coaching will assume the soil is OK and ready for planting in, and an NLP coach will support the gardener to achieve their dream of having a garden full of sunflowers by next summer.

The therapist will help the gardener dig over the soil first, take out all the stones, analyse the soil quality and make sure the ground is thoroughly prepared and weed free before planting the seeds.

As a gardener, I know both methods have their place – it is perfectly possible to plant the seeds without any soil preparation and nurture those seeds as they grow, watering them and pulling up the small weeds as they appear. And this is all which is needed to achieve a beautiful garden full of sunflowers, because the soil was healthy and ready to grow seeds.

Sometimes, it really doesn't matter how well the seeds are nurtured, the sunflower seeds do not grow tall and straight because there is something lurking in the soil which prevents this from happening. The soil looked fine when we started, but something is affecting the progress of the seeds.

Sometimes, NLP and coaching can quite easily deal with the something by clearing the limiting belief or asking powerful questions. And sometimes, regardless of our own and our client's capabilities, we do need to call in the soil expert.

Some of the confusion surrounding NLP and whether or not one is qualified as a therapist stems from the modelling projects first undertaken by Richard Bandler and John Grinder. Bandler and Grinder modelled therapists – Virginia Satir, the psychotherapist responsible for introducing family therapy; Fritz Perls, the psychiatrist and psychotherapist who introduced gestalt therapy; and Milton Erickson, a psychiatrist who had a big influence on hypnosis and family therapy.

Bandler and Grinder used these models to demonstrate if the strategies used by therapists were broken down enough into their constituent parts, then it was possible to replicate some of the results achieved by these therapists, i.e. they demonstrated the art of modelling excellence.

It is perfectly possible to achieve great results modelling the excellence of therapists and this is what makes NLP so effective in many different areas. NLP has been greatly influenced by the work of these successful therapists and is all about modelling some of the excellent strategies used by therapists in order to achieve results. This is not the same as saying you are a therapist.

There are many other elements which are required in order to qualify as a therapist, in just the same way as there are many other elements required to turn me into as successful a runner as Roger Bannister, the first person to run a 4 minute mile. – I can model his strategies and work out the 'difference that makes the difference', and this will, I am sure, improve my average times for running a mile. I do also need some other things in order to be at the next Olympics, standing next to the other athletes in the final – peak fitness levels, training and some initial talent would certainly help.

To clarify, as far as the Association for NLP is concerned, obtaining an NLP certificate only qualifies you as an NLP therapist when you have met the rigorous requirements of United Kingdom Council for Psychotherapy (UKCP), the British Association for Counselling and Psychotherapy (BACP) or the Neuro-Linguistic Psychotherapy and Counselling Association (NLPtCA). The UKCP website states: 'NLP techniques are often utilised to instigate change and enhance personal growth, development and performance in groups and organisations, and with individuals. NLP techniques are not always suitable in addressing complex psychological difficulties or distress.'

This is an understandable statement when you consider to qualify as an NLP Practitioner usually takes somewhere between 50 and 125 hours and will usually include a combination of study and practice. To qualify as an NLP psychotherapist takes over 2,300 hours and includes a combination of training, supervision, client contact, observation and self directed learning ... of which only a small part is achieving Practitioner and Master Practitioner qualifications.[1]

It is perfectly possible to add your NLP qualification to your existing therapist qualifications, in order to enhance your existing therapeutic practice. I know of many NLP Practitioners who use their NLP to enhance their specific qualifications as a GP, a psychologist, or a psychiatrist, and many others who have undertaken the rigorous training to qualify as a NLP psychotherapist. These people all use their NLP to enhance their existing knowledge and skills and thereby give an even better and more rounded service to their patients.

TIP *Be clear about what your own NLP qualifications enable you to do in practice. If you would like further clarification, talk to your trainer or contact ANLP for impartial advice.*

Another question which is frequently debated is: 'Can NLP practitioners ever do harm?'

I know coaching and NLP work on the basic assumption the client is whole and well, rather than broken in any way, and all we need to do is help them to find the resources they need, and already have within them, in order to make the changes they want to make.

[1] Source of hours - http://www.hypnotherapy-training.co.uk/ukcp-accreditation.php.

Is this basic assumption *always* true? Does this apply to every client we ever take on? Or is this assumption sometimes a convenient one to make in order to justify our actions as the coach? Is it ever possible to cause harm using NLP or coaching?

These questions were raised at a regulation debate in a coaching forum, and the view was very much coaching could never cause harm to others. Personally, having given these questions a great deal of thought, I think it is possible to do more harm than good on some occasions with some clients using both NLP and coaching.

Could it ever be possible to ask a powerful coaching question, which a client continues to deeply process after their coaching session, and which could lead to unforeseen consequences?

We had a call into the office one day, from someone who wanted some help but was not sure what to do or where to go. I assumed this was just another call from someone wanting a list of practitioners in their area, so started down this conversational route, which we have quite regularly with callers.

This caller was quite insistent he went to an experienced Master Practitioner because he had already been to see a Practitioner who had successfully dealt with his initial issue. He was convinced as a result of seeing this Practitioner, he had now developed agoraphobia and he wanted to see a more experienced NLP Practitioner in order to get rid of this.

Now I suspect what had happened in this case is the caller had some serious underlying issue or traumatic event, deeply hidden in his unconscious, and over the years he had put various strategies in place to effectively deal with this trauma and enable him to get on with life. The NLP Practitioner had successfully helped the client to remove these strategies, at which point the client had had to find some new extreme strategies, very quickly, to cover up what had been uncovered…so he became agoraphobic.

This is an extreme example and many people successfully utilise NLP on a daily basis to successfully support their clients through change. The point is it is important to be aware of the impact NLP can have, and take responsibility for ensuring you use your skills wisely.

NLP Professionals will always have a good awareness of their scope of practice and which clients they can realistically take on.

TIP

Instead of using terms like NLP Therapist to describe your role, use 'NLP Professional', or 'Educationalist' or 'Consultant', depending on the context of your particular business.

Ethics in practice

Professional ethics can, on one level, encompass a Code of Ethics, Code of Conduct and Code of Practice...and sometimes all three.[2]

However, within NLP, there are certain additional ethical codes in play, which are relevant and significant in the field of NLP, because we are, by the very nature of our subject, more aware of language. In my opinion, these additional ethics fall broadly into two categories:

▼ *Ethics around misrepresenting qualifications.*
▼ *Ethics around use of misleading language.*

Ethics around misrepresenting qualifications

What NLP does do well is model the qualification structure used by some other professions and make good use of the language around certification and qualification, which can potentially be misleading and cause confusion, especially with the general public.[3]

---

[2] ANLP Code of Ethics - http://www.anlp.org/members-code-of-ethics.

[3] NLP Qualifications Structure - http://www.anlp.org/nlp-qualifications-structure.

For example, in NLP, the most basic qualification we have is a Diploma – this usually equates to between two and four days' training in NLP and is often a precursor to a full Practitioner training. However, in the higher education system, there is a Higher Diploma in Education, which is achieved after one year full time or two years' part time study. A qualified teacher can then put 'Dip. Ed' after their name.

Unfortunately, it has been known for holders of a Diploma certificate in NLP to put 'Dip. NLP' after their name. This is blatant exploitation of the qualifications system and uses a minor qualification in NLP to imply something far greater than it really is.

I do know of one NLP trainer who asked a student to leave his course when he discovered the main reason for them being there was so they could do the minimum amount of training and then use the abbreviation 'Dip. NLP' after their name, to imply a full academic qualification.

We can take this further – once qualified as a Master Practitioner in NLP, I have seen instances where this has been abbreviated to 'Master's' – 'I have a Master's in NLP' or 'I am qualified to Master's level in NLP'. Again, within the higher education system, a Master's degree is a post graduate degree which can be achieved by a number of different routes, and usually involves a further one or two years' study after spending three years as an undergraduate to achieve a first degree.

Compare this to the amount of study time required to become an NLP Master Practitioner – it is possible to achieve a Master Practitioner certificate after only 130 hours of training (50 for Practitioner and 80 for Master Practitioner), and even the most rigorous NLP course will give you a certificate as a Master Practitioner after 300 hours of training (150 each for Practitioner and Master Practitioner). So a Master Practitioner qualification equates to between three and seven *weeks* of full time studying, as opposed to four or five *years* to achieve a Master's degree.

In many NLP training schools, but not all, it is also possible to become a Master Trainer of NLP, which is a level above NLP Trainer, and qualifies the practitioner to deliver NLP Trainers' training. This just adds further confusion because in NLP we have two other references to the word 'Master' (Master Practitioner and Master Trainer) which are sometimes interchanged and loosely used to imply the holder has a Master's degree in NLP.

As it is now possible to achieve an academic qualification in NLP (there are now Master's degree courses available at various UK universities), these interchangeable references to 'Master's' do allow some practitioners of NLP to misrepresent their qualifications to the public and use them to imply something they are not.

Some practitioners of NLP further confuse and potentially mislead the public by using acronyms in NLP to imply levels of qualifications. I have, at various times, seen practitioners using a whole string of acronyms after their name...for example:

Jim Bloggs, Dip. NLP, MBBNLP, MANLP, MABNLP, MTLT, MABH.

To a member of the public, who knows little about NLP, this looks even more impressive than:

Fred Smith, BSc, MD, FRCPS, FRS.

Yet Jim Bloggs' impressive string of acronyms actually means he has a Diploma in NLP (Dip. NLP), and is a member of: the British Board of NLP (BBNLP); the Association for NLP (ANLP); the American board of NLP (ABNLP); the Time Line therapy™ Association (TLT); and the American Board of Hypnotherapy (ABH). So Jim, despite his impressive title, has actually had four days training in NLP and paid to become a member of various professional bodies.

Fred Smith, on the other hand has a Bachelor of Science degree (BSc), is a Doctor of Medicine (MD), is a Fellow of the Royal College of Physicians and Surgeons (FRCPS) and is a Fellow of the Royal Society (FRS).

And if I chose, I could be:

Karen Moxom, BSc, MPNLP, FSP, RLTP, MFSB, MSEEE, HTC.

I have a Bachelor of Science degree (BSc), I am a Master Practitioner of NLP (MPNLP), I am a Feng Shui Practitioner (FSP), a Reiki Level 2 Practitioner (RLTP), a member of the Federation of Small Businesses (MFSB), a member of Social Enterprises East of England (MSEEE) and a holder of Tesco's Clubcard.

...it's a lot to live up to, and I think you understand my point.

> **TIP**
>
> *Look at how you convey your qualifications and memberships to your potential clients and ensure you are as clear as you can be with your own statements.*

Ethics around use of misleading language

It seems a few people are willing to go even further in their clever use of language to imply recognition or accreditation by one or more professional body, and thus attempt to further enhance their chances of picking up additional work and new clients. We have recently received complaints about the following clever use of wording on various websites.

'This course is recognised by ANLP, for membership' – technically this is correct, as the course is being delivered by a bona fide NLP Trainer, and any Practitioner course, provided it is delivered by a bona fide certified NLP trainer and is at least 50 hours, does mean the student is eligible for membership of ANLP... and it is still misleading to state this course is

recognised by ANLP, because this wording implies this Trainer has gone through some additional recognition/accreditation process in order to achieve special recognition.

'*A N Other is a well known trainer for ANLP*' – actually, A N Other is a member of ANLP. He pays his annual membership to belong to the association; he does not represent ANLP in any training capacity, nor does he train on our behalf, because ANLP does not run NLP trainings, its members do.

NLP does give us a greater understanding around language and the effects this can have on others. This is where NLP can be viewed as being manipulative, because as experts in the field of language, it could be argued any misleading statements made by an NLP practitioner are made intentionally and with full understanding of their intended consequences.

Where the power lies, for an NLP Professional, is in being able to do something with this understanding of language. Gemma Bailey is an NLP Professional who works with children, and very clearly describes how language can have a negative effect on a child. Gemma tells the story about how a seven-year-old was having problems with her peers and her school work, following the death of her grandfather.

When she was asked what was making school work tricky now, she replied she had lost her confidence...because Mummy had told her she had. Even though she had no idea what confidence was, what it looked, sounded or felt like, being told she had lost confidence was having a huge impact on this child's life.

I experienced something similar when I was in hospital a few years ago. I was due to have an operation which had been scheduled for months and was fairly routine day surgery... which meant I would go into hospital, have the operation and then be allocated a bed in a ward afterwards. So there we all sat, in the waiting room, just like a normal GP appointment.

In turn, we each got called in to see our surgeon for a pre-op check. Over the months, I had got well used to putting my own filters in place, and I would choose to modify the language of the medics before it reached me. So when they told me 'you will get these side effects', I heard 'you *may possibly* get some side effects'. When they listed all the risks of the operation and the anaesthetic, I heard about the *potential* risks.

There was another elderly lady who was scheduled to have an operation the same day, and she was sitting with her sister in the waiting room. I don't know what surgery she was having, but I did understand it was a minor procedure and she had been fairly relaxed, chatting happily to her sister since they had arrived, some two hours earlier.

She duly went into her pre-op interview, and presumably had a similar conversation with her surgeon to the one I experienced. She didn't have the benefit of putting the filters in place first, so she returned from her interview and walked slowly back to her place with her shoulders slouched. She slumped back down into her chair, turned to her sister and said, 'Well, that's it then, I'm going to die'.

If only the medics had fully understood the effects of the language they were using, then perhaps they could have modified it themselves. This way, those who don't understand the effect of their language could have been better cushioned in this situation...and more able to enjoy the benefits of approaching their operation with a slightly more positive frame of mind.

NLP Professionals already understand the effects language can have, which is why they will always consider the impact of their claims regarding qualifications, experience and achievements, ensuring these are accurately represented and never misleading.

In the long run, this manipulation of language to imply things can backfire, and we are seeing an increase in cases being brought by Trading Standards when the public complain they are being misled. This does nothing to enhance your reputation or the reputation of NLP…more on this in Chapter 7.

The recent changes in regulation by the Advertising Standards Authority (ASA), means their remit has now widened to include websites.[4] This means practitioners of NLP who do imply or make claims about their competence, do now have an extra layer of regulation to comply with, especially in the field of health and wellbeing.

The ASA's remit has been extended to ensure advertising and marketing materials on websites, as with other advertising, is decent, legal, honest and truthful. In other words, it is recognised businesses are using misleading language to make various claims, and now the weight of the Government has stepped in to protect the public.

This is actually good news for NLP Professionals, because it means those practitioners who do make far reaching claims about their services, do now have an authority to answer to. The downside is many bona fide practitioners of personal development methodologies such as NLP, Coaching and Hypnotherapy could fall foul of inflexible and stringently applied legislation.

Adopting minimum standards of practice

Another thing which all recognised professions have, and which NLP Professionals could choose to model, is having a set of minimum standards for practice. Many professions have a core set of standards and ethics they follow in order to practice safely.

Probably the most well known standard of practice is the Hippocratic Oath, which is commonly summed up as 'I will do my best to keep my patient from harm and is widely attributed to the medical profession (although not actually required by

[4] ASA - www.asa.org.uk.

many medical schools nowadays). Although this was written in 400 BC, it reflects a set of common principles for practice and does, I suspect, form the foundation of many codes of ethics in use today.[5]

It is wise, at this point, to look at the difference between 'standards' and 'standardisation', because I think sometimes, the two are confused and NLP practitioners sometimes perceive the whole topic of standards as restrictive and stifling flexibility and creativity (which goes against the whole ethos of NLP).

According to the Collins dictionary and thesaurus, a *'standard'* is a principle of propriety, honesty and integrity, a level of excellence or quality – something which presumably, all professionals would like to be associated with?

'Standardisation' on the other hand, is an attempt to regiment, i.e. to force discipline or order, especially in a domineering manner, which is both restrictive and stifling. This is something I personally would baulk at if applied to NLP and I am sure most other people would as well.

So adopting a common set of standards relating to best practice in NLP could create a greater sense of propriety, honesty and integrity within the profession and define a level of excellence or quality. Now wouldn't this be useful, and couldn't encouraging the further development of these standards and adoption of them across the field of NLP actually enhance your practice as an NLP Professional?

Realistic representation of NLP as a solution

NLP can be hugely empowering, especially when we realise we have a choice about our emotions and about how we choose to feel, think and do. NLP can have an important part to play in our lives and in the lives of others.

NLP has a relevant and positive part to play in many health related situations...and it is not a cure all. NLP can be effectively used on its own, in many situations and there are times when it can act as a complementary and supportive treatment alongside other, more conventional tools. It is, therefore, really important to be realistic about how and when NLP can be effective.

An acquaintance used many complementary treatments in her battle against cancer, which she did eventually lose. Sometimes, it seemed she may have used these more holistic approaches as alternatives rather than to complement more conventional medical interventions, and perhaps a more balanced approach may have yielded different results. We will never know whether the outcome would have been any different had she more successfully balanced conventional and complementary methods.

Rosie O'Hara, on the other hand, did embrace both NLP and conventional approaches when she was diagnosed with breast cancer in 2009. She wrote a touching and frank account of her experience for *Rapport* and has since written a book, *No More Bingo Dresses*.[6] She explained how various NLP skills had come into play from the moment she received her diagnosis, and how she used both NLP and allopathic medicine to overcome her illness more effectively.

Any client does need to be willing and ready for NLP to be effective in the first place. However much we want our client to change, whatever benefits we can see for our client, they are the only ones who can take the action and make the necessary changes.

We do get calls from people asking if NLP will work for them, and wanting some sort of guarantee to state after NLP has been done to them, their issues will be resolved. The client does have to be an active and willing participant in the game, rather than a spectator. The NLP Professional is the coach, rather than the player so realistically, it doesn't matter how good we are, if the client isn't engaging with the process, it is less likely to be successful.

---

[6] O'Hara, R. *No More Bingo Dresses: using NLP to cope with breast cancer and other people.* London; MX Publishing, 2011.

Fifty per cent of the problem is actually acknowledging there is an issue and taking enough responsibility to do something about it. Courts can send offenders to drug rehabilitation centres and alcoholism clinics, but unless the offender actually takes some responsibility for their own wellbeing, they may well re-offend.

We were burgled a few years ago and actually caught the offender still in the house. He pleaded not guilty for various reasons, but changed his plea when it came to court, and asked for a number of other offences to be taken into account. It then transpired he also had in excess of 40 previous convictions, most of which were fuelled by his drug habit.

He was given drug rehabilitation again, as well as a custodial sentence, and I wonder, at what point will he choose another path to follow? If he was willing to listen, then this is where NLP could play a valuable part in his rehabilitation, even if it were simply to engage with him for long enough to pace and lead him to a point where he was open to other possibilities.

Referral systems

If NLP were to more closely model best practice adopted by other professions, then NLP practitioners would have a client referral system in place.

Medical General Practitioners (GPs) have a referral system in place, which they will call upon as soon as their assessment of the situation indicates specialist help is required. We know, and expect, this service from our GP and we trust them, as professionals in their field, to know what they can deal with themselves and what they will refer on to another professional.

As a management accountant and trainer, I knew my scope of practice and area of expertise was in preparing management accounts and training others to do the same. I had initially trained with a firm of accountants so there was always someone to call upon who knew about the things I didn't.

As my experience grew, I did learn some basics in tax planning, auditing, trusts and strategic planning, and yet, when I became self-employed I was very aware of my boundaries of responsibility and expertise. I knew what I could generally deal with and I knew when I could stretch my boundaries and experience by taking on something which would challenge me, without compromising my clients...and I always had other professionals I could refer my clients on to for specialist advice.

It is so easy for us to sometimes believe we can solve every issue using NLP, and it is completely understandable we would want to, given our desire to help and support our clients. I once had a conversation with an NLP Practitioner who was excited because they had just been approached by someone who had obsessive compulsive disorder (OCD) and had heard NLP could help.

This Practitioner was enthusiastic and eager to help, newly qualified, had no prior experience with psychological disorders, and no system in place for referring on clients who may prove to be a little more challenging than they could cope with.

Despite this, they were going to take on the client because it was 'a useful experience and could be an interesting challenge'. An interesting challenge for whom, exactly? It is one thing to stretch ourselves and test ourselves in challenging situations – after all how else could we grow and gain new experiences. It is quite another to take on a client presenting something which we know to be outside our scope of practice, with no safety net in place, simply because it could be interesting.

So perhaps, when adopting a professional mindset, it is useful to consider whether or not the service you are providing is the best possible service for your client.

> TIP
>
> *Make it your business to get to know other helping professionals in your area, so you can build your own local database for referring clients.*

Coaching, mentoring and supervision

In effect, having your own coach, mentor or supervisor comes back down to walking your talk. If you are proposing your services can support people to make lasting and significant changes to their lives, doesn't it follow you may also need support in your journey as an NLP professional?

The field of NLP is a subjective one, and by its very nature, does 'mess with people's heads'. NLP language is supposed to challenge our thinking patterns and potentially alter our beliefs, opening up new opportunities and choices for future consideration.

You may find at various stages in your NLP career you need different levels of coaching, mentoring or supervision. As a newly qualified practitioner I would have welcomed some mentoring and supervision, so I had someone more experienced than me to share my concerns or client experiences with. I really did feel, on occasions I would appreciate the input from someone more experienced to offer guidance and suggestions.

I currently have a marketing coach and a business mentor, and both provide an invaluable service, enabling me to move forward and holding me to account in just the same way you might do with your own clients.

> TIP
>
> *Walk your talk and get your own coach, mentor or supervisor.*

Continual professional development

Many professions nowadays recognise the value of undertaking continual professional development (CPD). Certainly, I would suggest in the ever evolving world of NLP, CPD is a good professional model to adopt and some of the professional bodies, including ANLP, have introduced guidelines.

The essence of NLP is about modelling excellence, and because of this, it is continually evolving and reshaping itself. So if we want to deliver the best service possible to our clients, and ensure those models we learned about 10 years previously are still working, we owe it to ourselves and our clients to continue to professionally develop ourselves and refresh our learnings and skills on a regular basis.

There are different CPD models currently available, and the most commonly recognised one is completing a set number of additional hours training every year. There is a move, however, in some professions, towards reflective learning as a basis for CPD.

After all, it is possible to turn up at a conference or workshop, obtain your CPD certificate declaring you have attended an 8 hour conference…and then you could, if you really wanted to, sit in the coffee bar for three hours (which I did do once because the workshop was, in my opinion, rubbish.). The workshop attendance model only works well if you have a lot of money to spend on additional courses.

The reflective learning model of CPD is far more flexible (you can probably tell I like flexibility.). Any form of learning can be incorporated in this model, which means it is far more accessible and affordable for any professional. Because its basis is one of reflecting on what you have learned, and how this could impact on your business, your clients, your own self development, then many different learnings can be incorporated in this model – reading a relevant book, attending a practice group, having a useful, educative discussion with a colleague or supervisor. All these activities can be reflected upon and their impact on your business can be measured and recorded.

This model is becoming more recognised, and is already adopted by some of the caring professions such as nurses and radiographers, where it is not simply a question of acquiring more knowledge about your subject, it's also about applying these skills to improve your practices. ANLP also model this approach to CPD, and more NLP and coaching training schools are moving towards this standard of practice for NLP.

To quote Peter Drucker: 'Follow effective action with quiet reflection. From the quiet reflection will come even more effective action.'

TIP

Keep your own knowledge up to date by undertaking regular CPD – this can be as simple as attending a Practice Group or reading a relevant book.

Summary

Best practice in other professions can include an awareness of your scope of practice standards and ethics, realistic representation of NLP as a potential solution, having appropriate referral systems on place, having your own coach, mentor or supervisor and undertaking continual professional development.

As well as increasing your own credibility as an NLP Professional, adopting the principles of best practice will certainly add to the credibility of the field of NLP, which ultimately contributes to NLP being recognised as a credible profession and your demand, as an NLP Professional, increasing as a result.

Demonstrate best practice

CHAPTER FOUR

Appreciating the Value of Social Proof

*'Any fact is better established
by two or three testimonies
than by a thousand arguments.'*

Marie Dressler, actress (1869–1934)

Wikipedia defines social proof, or informational social influence, as a 'psychological phenomenon where people assume the actions of others reflect correct behaviour for a given situation. This effect is prominent in ambiguous social situations where people are unable to determine the appropriate mode of behaviour, and is driven by the assumption that surrounding people possess more knowledge about the situation.'[1]

NLP could certainly be defined as ambiguous and therefore does lend itself to being one of those professions which could benefit from gathering more social proof on every level, especially if NLP were ever to become regulated at some point in the future.

Many practitioners of NLP claim 'NLP works' and this statement should be good enough to persuade people to part with their hard earned cash. To believe NLP can become a successful and accepted profession simply based upon opinion, with no supporting evidence to back this up, is both arrogant and naive.

NLP Professionals appreciate the value of having evidence to support their claims, because they understand potential clients may be looking at a variety of solutions to their particular issue and they need to evaluate and compare the options available.

NLP Professionals accept to operate in the real world, they need to match the expectations of their potential clients. They know social proof is a powerful way of pacing and leading a potential client and converting them into a paying client.

With the recent regulatory changes in the Advertising Standards Authority (ASA) remit, however, social proof requirements have been taken to a whole new level – supporting evidence for claims has now taken on a whole new meaning and NLP, like many other helping professions, has to move forward with obtaining evidence to prove its claims.

Realistically, the NLP profession cannot produce the body of evidence required by the ASA overnight – their requirements are rigorous, detailed and are necessary for each of the medical conditions in which NLP can be used with good effect. These conditions include 'feeling down or feeling blue', aches and pains, confidence, fears and phobias, stress, guilt and smoking cessation.

The recent changes to the ASA remit could just be the beginning, as far as regulation and the impact it could have on NLP. So, before we get into the value of social proof, let's address the whole debate around potential regulation.

At the moment, coaching and NLP are unregulated and the debate surrounding potential regulation is a controversial topic.

Why would anyone want to regulate NLP in the first place? Well, I have probably already answered this question by illustrating not everyone has the same level of responsibility towards their NLP and coaching practices, in just the same way not everyone has the same attitude towards driving.

We are all individuals and across the range there will be some very diverse approaches to driving, with some of us managing to get through our entire driving career without so much as a parking ticket or speeding fine, whereas others may end up being jailed or banned for careless driving...and most of us are somewhere in between.

We do have wide ranging driving laws in the UK, which are designed to ensure the safety of every individual on the road and everyone we may come into contact with whilst on the road. Sometimes, we may perceive these laws as being restrictive or plain ridiculous on occasions, and yet their intention is usually to protect us – this is the positive intention behind regulation.

The challenge with regulation is sometimes, in an attempt to protect the public from a few irresponsible individuals, there does often seem to be an extreme attitude.

Even though NLP and coaching are not specifically regulated, there are already laws and regulations in place which do affect us as NLP practitioners and which are designed to protect the public. As well as the Children's Act, the Vetting and Barring Scheme is likely to find its way into statute sooner or later, and this will mean it will be compulsory for anyone working with children or vulnerable adults to be registered. Vulnerable adults does include anyone with a mental health condition including anxiety or depression, so may already cover some of your clients.

TIP

Make sure you are working within existing legislation for your area of expertise (www.legislation.gov.uk).

The Council for Healthcare Regulatory Excellence (CHRE) has now been appointed as the regulator for psychotherapists and counsellors and will be looking at quality assured self regulation. The CHRE website states they 'promote the health and well being of patients and the public in the regulation of health professionals.[2]

If this is the case, and regulation for psychotherapists and counsellors is already in the pipeline, then I think it would be a good idea for NLP Practitioners to at least investigate how we could be best prepared for this opportunity. At the moment, regulation for NLP Practitioners is a choice, i.e. there is no specific statutory regulation, so we currently have the opportunity to be curious about the options and explore how we could best work with them.

We have an opportunity to demonstrate, as a profession, we can take responsibility for ourselves and have in place good systems for encouraging self responsibility. We can demonstrate we already adhere to standards of best practice, we take responsibility for the continued development of our skills, we recognise our scope of practice and we have systems in place to deal with unexpected outcomes.

This way, if regulation is introduced at a later date, because we have demonstrated we are already acting responsibly, any regulation could be more sympathetic with a lighter touch approach, simply because we have demonstrated we already have good self regulatory systems in place.

Alternatively, we can continue to ignore the possibility of regulation, preferring instead to take a more maverick approach which means we can continue to do what we like and when we like, with no accountability to others. This is not quite true and most of us would run a basic ecology check – whilst NLP is empowering in this respect, and enlightens us to the options and choices we have, I would like to believe we are still operating within the basic rules of society and having some respect for another person's model of the world.

As with all laws and regulations, if we are staying within these boundaries anyway, then they will not actually affect our

[2] Council for Healthcare Regulatory Excellence (CHRE) website, http:www.chre.org.uk.

practice. If we already have effective self regulatory boundaries in place then it is only those who stray from these boundaries who need to be concerned.

There are many laws in the UK, which have no effect on my life whatsoever because my own standards of behaviour mean I am living within those boundaries anyway. It is only when I am straying close to the statutory boundaries (like keeping to the 30 mile limit on an open road near our office), I then become aware and do need to consciously make the effort to work within the existing regulations.

I was driving in Hampshire recently and saw warning sign for livestock in road (at the same time as I drove across a cattle grid)...seconds later I came across a few horses, grazing at the road side. This got me thinking – these horses were contained within a boundary (cattle grids and fences) and yet they were enjoying plenty of freedom within these boundaries and even though they have the capability to jump the fence and run off into the wild, they choose not to.

So if the horses running wild in the New Forest is a metaphor for the freedom from regulation currently enjoyed by the NLP community, what would happen if someone on the council decided these horses need to be reined in and penned (for their own safety as well as safety of others)?

If this did happen, my preference would be to start looking at the type of fencing and the layout of the fencing, and investigate how we can influence where the fencing gets put, rather than trotting off to Dartmoor and hoping their local council has a more lenient attitude towards wild horses.

What is important in any regulation debate is we have a voice at the table; we have the opportunity to put our point of view across and to be recognised and heard in case the debate about potential regulation starts to become a reality.

I propose therefore, it would be a good idea to make some decisions as a profession and take steps to get our own house in order. This way, we are prepared for what may (or may not) happen and we have taken steps to demonstrate our own sense of responsibility whilst we do still have a choice in the matter.

The National Autistic Society (NAS) were successful in getting the first specific autism bill through parliament recently, because they were at the table, representing their members and their families, and were able to speak with authority about how people with autism are affected in every day society.

The same is true for NLP – when it comes to issues such as regulation, standards and legislation, the 30,000 plus qualified NLP Practitioners in the UK are not going to be individually and personally invited, by the government or the potential regulators, to come and have a chat about how regulation could affect them and their business.

What the government and regulators will want to do is engage with the professional bodies and trade associations which represent the views of their members. It is much easier and more practical for them to talk to a small group of people who represent their profession, rather than engage with every person in the profession individually. In fact, the HPC (Health Professions Council) state any profession needs to 'have at least one established professional body which accounts for a significant proportion of that occupational group.'

This is exactly what the Committee of Advertising Practice (CAP)[3] did with regard to the new ASA remit – they were happy to work with us to provide guidelines for our members, rather than have to deal individually with a number of NLP professionals.

Apart from the ASA remit, potential regulation for NLP is still something for us to consider at some time in the future. Putting the ASA evidence requirements and regulation to one

[3] www.cap.org.uk.

side for a moment, supporting evidence in NLP forms part of our need for social proof now as well as to prepare us for the future. For NLP Professionals, credible forms of social proof can include:

▼ *Research.*

▼ *Third party accreditation.*

▼ *Personal testimonials.*

▼ *Professional memberships.*

Research

Whilst academic research may seem to be very robust, standardised and rigorous, it is essential if we are to ever have NLP acknowledged as a viable helping profession, even in the eyes of the ASA. NLP research, even the type which is not necessarily recognised as robust enough by the ASA,[4] plays a valuable role in raising awareness and adding to the credibility of NLP.

Scepticism does exist, especially in the health, education and some business sectors. Health and educational practitioners frequently require evidence something works. Whilst the average man in the street or small business has the autonomy to make their own decisions, many larger organisations, education authorities and primary care trusts have to be able to justify their proposed investment in an NLP practitioner.

We would be appalled if the NHS were to approve a new drug for general release without ensuring it had been rigorously tested first, and there was evidence to ensure every aspect of the new drug's performance had been checked and passed as safe.

Testimonials, success stories and case studies do give subjective accounts of how NLP has worked for a particular individual or with a particular issue, but these, in themselves,

---

[4] ASA substantiation requirements - http//:www.anlp.org/files/asa-substantiation-guidelines_38_181.pdf.

are not likely to be enough to sway a board of NHS professionals, who are making decisions about how best to allocate their health budget for the coming year.

We trust our GP to recommend only what is safe and what will work, and you can imagine what could happen if they were to prescribe a drug purely on the basis their mother-in-law's neighbour's cousin had tried it and reported it was 'quite good'.

There are levels of research which are acceptable and not all research does have to be academically rigorous. Cognitive behavioural therapy (CBT) is widely recognised within the NHS and one of the main reasons for this is because they record their results, and therefore have evidence a patient has made progress.

In NLP, we do measure results as well, otherwise how would we know when a client has reached their outcome? We are all taught about SMART goals and the 'M' stands for measurable. How many times have you said to a client, before their NLP coaching: 'On a scale of 1 to 10, how do you feel about [your challenge] at the moment?'

And then once you have completed the NLP intervention or coaching session, you will ask the same question, so both you and your client can get an idea of where they are now with regard to their particular challenge.

So I would suggest as far as measuring and recording results is concerned, the only difference between NLP and CBT is we don't record the patient feedback, which we are already measuring, or complete questionnaires to demonstrate progress.

At a very basic level, how simple could it be to start monitoring the before and after progress of our clients and then record this information, with a variety of clients over a set time period… and then have some evidence your interventions have made a measurable difference.

Ellie Moseley, a recruitment consultant and NLP Practitioner did just this as part of her modelling project. She modelled more successful recruitment consultants and noticed what they did to create their success (we know about modelling, so I don't need to explain further). By modelling a few successful recruitment consultants, rather than just one, she was able to obtain a sample of results and justify her findings for her project, based on the fact she had a sample of data and similar behaviours had been noticed across a range of successful consultants.

The true academics may argue Ellie's research was not academically robust, and yet she had taken the time to record and analyse her results. We published her findings in *Rapport* and weeks later, Ellie contacted me to say, 'As a result things have really kicked off at work and I am really in demand with the training team'.

...so this worked well then.

TIP

Start recording some of your own before and after scores for a range of interventions you undertake with clients. At least you are starting to gather some evidence of your effectiveness as an NLP Professional.

There are ways of challenging, testing and recording what we do, regardless of the fact there is a lot of subjectivity involved. Academic research can be dismissed both within and outside the NLP community for this reason.

Quite often, NLP practitioners will argue because NLP is so subjective, it cannot be formally and robustly researched in any way, as NLP methods cannot be measured in academically robust ways. I am sure I remember learning in NLP 'cannot' is simply another choice – we 'can' choose to 'not' do something?

NLP Master Trainer and friend, Melody Cheal, researched and wrote her MSc Positive Psychology dissertation about the impact of NLP on self esteem and subjective wellbeing. She introduced plenty of well formed and justifiable reasons as to why wellbeing, despite being subjective, can be included and validated as a measure.[5]

The whole reason the International NLP Research Conference[6] was set up, was to initiate some valid enquiries into NLP and start to find a body of evidence to (hopefully) support and evidence our claims 'NLP works'. The 'hopefully' is significant because in order to prove the validity of NLP, it is important to take those risks and be prepared to challenge the claims made by NLP practitioners.

At the very least, to be taken seriously we do need to have enough confidence in our own area of expertise (NLP) to be willing to challenge the claims we make.

The NLP Research Conference has become an established event in the NLP profession and its vision is: 'To further develop the International NLP Research Conference, so it becomes the number one internationally recognised Research Platform for NLP, and through this establish NLP as a more accessible, credible and evidence based profession.'

The conference aims are straight forward and simple:

▼ *To further develop the discipline of NLP as a field of theory, research and practice.*

▼ *To provide a credible platform for supporting and promoting NLP Research across the globe.*

▼ *To establish* Current Research in NLP *as an internationally recognised, credible, academically peer reviewed journal for NLP research.*

---

[5] NLP Positive Psychology dissertation pdf at http://www.gwiztraining.com/NLP%20Positive%20 Psychology%20Dissertation.pdf.

[6] NLP Research Conference at http://www.nlpresearchconference.com.

▼ *To provide a dissemination forum for empirical and practical research in NLP.*

▼ *To disseminate research through publication in* Current Research in NLP, *the first international, academically peer reviewed journal for NLP research.*

▼ *To facilitate a partnership between NLP practitioners and academics and enable research to take place across the field of NLP.*

Current Research in NLP the peer reviewed academic journal published following the Research Conference, does contain academically robust and rigorous papers about the applications of NLP in various settings, specifically education, psychology and business.

There are NLP research projects happening all over the UK and abroad. The CfBT Education Trust publishes research specific to the education sector and has supported and published powerful NLP related research.[7] This research will help teachers and educational establishments make favourable decisions regarding the inclusion of NLP in their training programmes.

Frank Bourke leads the NLP Research and Recognition project in the USA.[8] One of their aims is to secure funding for NLP research projects and collate a resources library of NLP research.

To be honest, could the research aspect of NLP go some way towards raising its credibility with the wider public, by being seen to question and challenge aspects of NLP, and by evidencing, disproving and validating the work we do?

Asking questions, reframing and challenging beliefs is what we do, so I would encourage some openness and a degree of

---

[7] Carey, J., Churches, R., Hutchinson, G., Jones, J. and Tosey, P. 'Neuro-linguistic programming and learning: teacher case studies on the impact of NLP in education', CfTB - http://www.anlp.org/files/cfbt-education-research-2010_6_82.pdf.

[8] www.nlprandr.org.

willingness around putting NLP through the same process which we put our clients.

We have processes in place to test our clients' responses and we know all about behavioural strategies. A lot of human behaviour uses a strategy called the TOTE model (Test, Operate, Test, Exit) and we do already apply these strategies to NLP as a subjective experience in the same way we apply them to other areas of our lives.

We would also expect this model to be applied to most aspects of our own business, so it seems reasonable to apply it to NLP...and simply record our results. We apply these principles to our own business, and the health and education systems certainly apply this strategy, so all we would be doing is providing them with the written evidence we have done the same with NLP.

This may not be the robustness academic research offers, and it is a start. Collecting evidence to demonstrate what we do does work will start to bridge the gap between academic research and the well known, but unacceptable phrase 'well... it works'.

After all, I may not need to understand how my car works or what the mechanic has to do to keep it roadworthy, but I am obliged to obtain the evidence to demonstrate my car works before I can get insurance and use it on the road (it's called an MOT certificate). It is not good enough for me to simply tell the authorities my car works. I have to provide proof it still works, every year, before I can get my car tax.

Third party accreditation

In Chapter 3, I referred to the ambiguous language sometimes used by NLP Practitioners. It is quite possible the reason this ambiguous language can sometimes be used, is because it is understood one of the things both the public and industry frequently do look for is some sort of external validation for courses and Practitioners.

The public hear all sorts of negative stories in the press and as NLP is unregulated, they do seek some sort of reassurance what they are about to invest in has been accredited, approved or recognised by a third party.

It is a requirement for many areas of the public sector for workshops and courses to have external accreditation. We have, in the past, had conversations with NLP practitioners and representatives from the police force, the armed forces, schools and even HM Revenue and Customs. These NLP Professionals are requesting third party verification for the courses they run, because this verification has been requested by their client. Representatives from the public sector are looking for courses which have been accredited or approved by an external body, as it is part of their internal policies to only run 'accredited courses' or hire in an 'approved professional'.

When you look at this from the potential client's point of view, this is an understandable reaction. Quite often, the person responsible for hiring in the services of a professional has all sorts of checking procedures to complete, in order to demonstrate they have completed their due diligence and can justify why they have hired in a particular practitioner to deliver training. Therefore, employing the services of a professional who does have some sort of external verification or accreditation for the courses they deliver can help with this process.

I know the depth of checks which sometimes have to be undertaken are rigorous, and rightly so. I am a school governor and a Scout helper, and because I am a volunteer, who may come into contact with some of the children on occasions, as part of the process, I had to undergo a Criminal Record Bureau (CRB) check.

As a parent, I would certainly expect the school to run these external checks and validations on any person coming into contact with my child, because they have a duty of care to me as a parent and they have a duty to ensure our children are safe when in their care.

Even individuals, who don't have to comply with company policy and procedures, often seek some sort of verification the person they are about to choose does have approval or recognition from someone else.

I recently had to purchase some new software for running our payroll. It is quite important to calculate payroll correctly – as employers we have a statutory duty to correctly calculate pay and deductions and report these to HM Revenue and Customs. We also have a responsibility to our employees to ensure we pay them correctly.

Rather than just searching for 'payroll software' on the internet, the first thing I did was go onto the HM Revenue and Customs' website and find their list of 'HMRC approved software' because I knew this would have already been checked and I would be better off, in the long run, investing in something which had already been validated. It also saved me a lot of time on due diligence, because if HM Revenue and Customs had already checked and approved this software, then I could presume it works and it already meets their criteria.

So it is quite easy to understand why some individuals and companies do seek external validation for the services they are buying – it is their investment in terms of time, money and energy, they do want some assurance their investment will be worth it, and by selecting something which has already been externally validated, they have completed some of their due diligence quickly and easily, and have some justification for their choice.

If you have designed a piece of payroll software, it is quite easy to work out where to get it externally verified so you have a better chance of selling your product. This is because there is only one government agency responsible for ensuring payrolls are correctly calculated and this is HMRC. But where does a coach or NLP practitioner go to get such approval, validation or accreditation?

Luckily, for those options orientated NLP practitioners, it just means you have more choice. For starters, you can choose whether or not you want to get external validation for your work, just as the software developer can choose whether or not they get their payroll software approved. If you do decide you want external verification for your services, workshops and courses, then there are many different ways you can go about this.

Depending on the sector in which you deliver your courses, you may find there is sector specific accreditation you can achieve. For example, if you are developing or wanting to deliver courses which relate to leadership and management, you can get accreditation or approval from the Institute for Leadership and Management (ILM).

Similarly, if you want your courses to have a more academic association, then some the universities and further education colleges are open to partnering with you to develop and deliver approved courses across a variety of subjects.

If you are a therapist, you would probably seek approval and recognition from the UK Council for Psychotherapy (UKCP) or Neuro-Linguistic Psychotherapy and Counselling Association (NLPtCA), who specialise in psychotherapy and counselling, and certainly if you wanted to become a psychotherapist, it would be wise to undertake a course which has UKCP approval.

All these accreditations and approvals cover a variety of techniques and skills which enhance the specialised subject they focus on. For example, the ILM will approve all qualifying courses which relate to leadership and management, as long as the skills being taught relate to leadership and management.

The alternative to sector specific approval is third party verification from one of the bodies which oversees the field in which you practice, i.e. coaching or NLP. This way, rather than having your specific courses recognised within the specialised sector in which you operate (i.e. leadership and management, academia, psychotherapy), you and all your courses can be recognised because they relate to NLP or coaching.

The Association for Coaching (AC) do offer accreditation for coaches, the International Coach Federation (ICF) offer 'independent credentialing' for coaches, and the Association for NLP (ANLP) offers accreditation for NLP professionals, their training courses and workshops. All these accreditations cover coaches and NLP practitioners from all walks of life and offer verification for your services as a coach or NLP practitioner, rather than your services to a specialised subject.

So, for example, if you use external validation and wanted to underpin all your courses, you could have all your work as an NLP Practitioner recognised by ANLP and all your work as a coach accredited by AC. As well as this, you could then opt to have your 'NLP for effective managers' course recognised by ILM and your psychotherapy training approved by UKCP.

We do get regular enquiries from members of the public, wanting to check whether a particular trainer is accredited with ANLP, or a certain course is recognised by ANLP. When the answer is 'no, this course is not ANLP accredited', we are usually asked to provide details of an ANLP Accredited course or trainer.

So to those who question the value of external accreditation and debate whether there is a need for any accrediting body in NLP, I would say there is a definite need indicated in the level of enquiries we get from your potential clients.

Do you need your work to be accredited by anyone else? My answer would be to ask what your potential clients are looking for in the way of credibility and reassurance and deliver what your clients are seeking.

My personal view as to whether or not accreditation has a place in NLP comes back to having flexibility and respect for another person's model of the world.

There is a demand for external accreditation, both from NLP practitioners and from their potential clients (especially in the public sector, health and education sectors). So if some Professionals wish to have their work independently checked and externally validated, they should be given the opportunity to achieve accreditation.

For those who don't believe in it or feel they don't need it, then it is OK – it is a choice. I do believe NLP Professionals, who understand the importance of social proof and external verification are more likely to have their work independently accredited and value the intangible benefits of accreditation.

TIP

Read this Marketing Week article on how brands are using accreditation to boost trust and profits: http://www. marketingweek.co.uk/in-depth-analysis/cover-stories/third-party-coalitions-get-seal-of-approval/3013602.article.

Personal testimonials

The simplest and quickest way to start collecting social proof and evidence to add credibility to the services you offer is by asking for testimonials from your clients.

You can do this right from the very first client you work with...or even with other students on your training course – after all, if you are able to help someone to resolve a challenge, even in a training room environment or with a pro bono client, it's a start.

I remember when I started my coaching programme, three of us set up a co-coaching group. This worked really well because there was always a coach, a client and an observer, who was able to comment on improvements. Not only were we practising and learning from each other, we also gave each other testimonials, which actually gave us all a boost of confidence as well as our first bit of social proof.

This works particularly well if you are delivering any pro bono coaching, either as part of your training or when you first start. Rather than offering something completely free, create some value for your services by asking for payment in the form of a testimonial.

As you start to collate your testimonials, you will find some of these naturally develop further into case studies, or success stories which you can use to demonstrate the effect your services are having on your clients.

TIP

The new ASA regulations do mean testimonials cannot be used to endorse a claim relating to one of the medical conditions referred to in this chapter. They are quite strict on what is and isn't allowed in terms of marketing so do check their guidelines (http://www.copyadvice.org.uk/ CAP-Code/CAP-Codes-Item.aspx?q=CAP%20Code%20new_ General%20Sections_03%20Misleading%20advertising_ Rules_Endorsements%20and%20Testimonials#c138) and we do provide some specific examples relating to NLP for members on our website (http://www.anlp.org/asa-guidelines-for-anlp-members).

Professional memberships

It would be a little remiss of me to be Managing Director of the Association for NLP and then not mention Professional Memberships in a book for NLP Professionals.

Seriously, one of the ways to demonstrate social proof is to belong to the Trade Associations or Professional Membership bodies relating to your area of expertise, whether this is NLP, Coaching, Hypnotherapy or Thought Field Therapy.

Professional Membership bodies provide practitioners with a form of self regulation and accountability for their profession, and most credible professions do have at least one Professional Body.

I would take a marketer who belongs to the Chartered Institute of Marketing (CIM) more seriously than a marketer who doesn't belong to any professional or trade association. When we were building our house, I always looked for trades who belonged to some professional association for extra reassurance. In fact, I used to check their membership association had a complaints process, so there was some form of redress should anything go wrong – I discovered the hard way it is a good idea to have every extra piece of reassurance possible.

We know from calls we receive in the office, your potential clients are thinking the same thing, and seeking the extra reassurance which comes from belonging to a Trade Association. For every person who calls the office enquiring about locating a practitioner in their area, we must get at least one call enquiring about whether a particular training company is registered with us. So the indications are your potential clients also give credence to whether or not you belong to your Professional Body or Trade Association.

Summary

Social proof is important for any emerging field, especially those, like NLP, which have some ambiguity around them. Social proof can include research, independent accreditation, testimonials and membership of professional bodies.

So how does all this potential social proof benefit you as a Professional and NLP as a field?

I believe without a body of evidence and social proof to prove its effectiveness, as legislation and regulation increases, NLP will be shelved in favour of other, more evidence based approaches which can offer proof to support their claims.

Appreciate the value of social proof

CHAPTER FIVE

Celebrating our Differences

*'For too long, we have focused on our differences –
in our politics and backgrounds, in our race
and beliefs – rather than cherishing the
unity and pride that binds us together.'*

Bob Riley, American politician (1944–)

NLP is a hugely diverse field of practice and sometimes, practitioners of NLP can get bogged down in the differences between themselves and their competitor. Quite often, these differences can hinge around the length of training programme or the particular style of training undertaken or offered.

It is quite common for these differences to be played out in the public arena because it is the only thing which differentiates your services from those of the NLP practitioner in the next town (or even the next street).

NLP Professionals understand the bigger picture and are able to chunk up...and chunk down again. NLP Professionals celebrate our differences, realising it is all about respecting other models of the world and accepting there are different training models for NLP – these all have a part to play in the developing field of NLP and the thing we all have in common is...NLP.

Diversity is healthy and allows you to stand out in your chosen profession . . . being different to your fellow practitioners of

NLP is one of the most powerful marketing tools you have and will make you stand out as an NLP Professional.

In order to recognise the value of NLP as a profession, and accept we all have a part to play in delivering NLP to the public, let's take an open minded look at the NLP community to which we all belong.

Chunking up...

It seems some NLP practitioners are keen to divide our community based upon our training lineage. The training lineage division has evolved for a number of reasons, one of which is based upon the number of hours you have trained in order to obtain your NLP Practitioner certificate (which ultimately relates back to who you trained with and which certification you obtained).

As long as I have been involved in NLP, there has been a debate around the number of hours one can train – 'full length' courses are around 20 days (125 hours) and 'shorter' courses are around 7 days (about 50 hours).

It is now possible to obtain an NLP Practitioner certificate without any face to face training at all. I am often asked to comment on the different lengths of courses, and I have been involved in many a debate about the quality, value and merit of short courses when compared with a longer length course.

I think both types of courses have their place within the NLP community and both can bring great value to the public and play a part in creating a positive impact within society. One of the presuppositions of NLP is all about respecting another person's model of the world – so couldn't this diversity mean we have found more than one way of delivering our NLP and this just emphasises our flexibility?

I do agree it is confusing someone who trains for 50 hours can obtain a Practitioner certificate, when someone else can train for 125 hours to also obtain a Practitioner certificate. There is currently no discernable difference between the two qualifications, given both people have qualified as NLP Practitioners.

This diverse practice is not unique to the field of NLP – it is the same at university. For one thing the most prestigious universities in the UK offer the same first degree qualification as one of the lesser universities...and now they can even charge the same tuition fees. It's not necessarily fair and it is what happens in the university system.

So yes, the current system for NLP can be misleading and unfair, and there is potential for further improvement, as my geography teacher would often write in my school report. This happens in every evolving field of study, and the fact we are in a position to contribute to this continuing evolution is a cause for celebration. We can contribute because the NLP community is a lot smaller than the education system, and currently our fate is more in our own hands.

NLP is subjective – we all agree on this. So learning about NLP is subjective too and presumably, only a part of this learning boils down to the number of hours we are taught. I have met many NLP practitioners from all lineages and I really do believe a good NLP practitioner is about so much more than the number of hours they were taught in the first place.

Put yourself in the shoes of a potential client for a moment... imagine you are looking for a NLP practitioner to help you with a particular challenge you are facing (content isn't important here).

What are you looking for in this practitioner? As a member of the public, are you really interested in whether they have qualified through the International NLP Trainers Association (INLPTA) or the Society of NLP (SNLP) or the International Training Association (ITA) or the American Board of NLP

(ABNLP) or the Professional Guild? In fact, do you, as a potential client, understand anything about the different lineages, never mind know the difference between INLPTA, SNLP, ITA and ABNLP?

Or are there other things which concern you more than where your practitioner obtained their qualification? I choose my GP based on many criteria, including recommendation, reputation, location and possibly even their appearance (!), but I have never chosen my GP based upon which college they attended.

As a member of the NLP community, *you* may be interested in where your colleagues trained – and what interests you within the NLP community is completely different to what interests a potential client.

It may be true within the GP community, the information about original training college is significant, and I am sure there is qualification snobbery in their profession, just as there is with universities and NLP ... and as time goes on, our experience and our ability to apply our learnings (as a GP, a graduate or an NLP practitioner) do take on more significance than where we trained.

TIP

Think about what your potential clients really want to know about you – they may be more interested in how you can help them solve their problem.

Can you recall the last time you completed your CV? You must have noticed as you got older (or you will notice as you get older) the experience section of your CV gets longer and the qualifications section becomes more abbreviated and summarised ... in my first CV, my qualifications listing was massive – I detailed every O level subject (and grade), my A levels, my degree and any other significant (or insignificant) certificate which I had ever achieved, including Grade 1 piano.

The last time I needed a CV, my qualifications list had changed considerably to a one line summary – I now simply had 10 O levels, 3 A levels and a degree ... and my prospective employer would never have even known about my stunning musical achievement because I needed the space on my CV to list all my subsequent experience and knowledge relevant to the job application.

So you see, when dealing with the world outside the NLP community (the world which contains all your potential clients), it is about so much more than your NLP lineage.

Remember one of the chunking up exercises you may have done whilst you were on your NLP training. I recall sitting with a partner, and being asked to say something factual about myself and what I did...and when I made this statement, my partner simply responded with something like, 'that's great... and you are so much more than that...what else are you?'

In a few short moments I went from being 'just an accountant' to being someone really superb, wonderful and awesome (for me, at least). This was a valuable lesson in chunking up and it does apply to us all – we are all so much more than the number of hours we trained or the NLP lineage we followed.

If we were to chunk up from our differences to find our shared perspective, it's quite easy to spot one of them is we all share a common interest – NLP.

We all know and understand the power of beliefs. We all know the effect unhelpful and limiting beliefs can have on our lives. At some point during your training, you either witnessed or personally experienced what can happen when one of those unhelpful, limiting beliefs is replaced by something which is more useful and works far more effectively.

When it comes to NLP, we are lucky, because we already all share some positive beliefs about the power of NLP, the difference it can make and the fact it works. This, in itself, is immensely empowering for us as individuals, for our colleagues and for the whole field of NLP. Imagine what could happen if we were to take those positive beliefs which reside within the community and really use them to celebrate our successes, which all come from some shared positive beliefs NLP can make a difference to others.

I can think of many other occasions when harnessing positive beliefs within a community works with amazing results. A friend came back from a trip to Rwanda and Uganda, where she had been part of a group helping the orphanages out there, as well as taking the opportunity to trek and explore the jungles and experience the wildlife of Africa.

She was telling me how well they gelled as a group and, even though they came from many varied and different backgrounds (and countries), they all shared some common beliefs about the trip, and had a common desire to help, learn and experience what was on offer. They used their common positive attitude to carry them through the trip, celebrating their successes (from helping a village football team, to hiking up a mountain and through the jungle to see gorillas) and supporting each other when things became challenging.

You may not have experienced anything quite so extreme, and I am sure you can think of occasions when the whole atmosphere is charged with a sense of positivity, when some shared beliefs and values really do light up the room...maybe at a wedding, or even during your NLP training?

We do already have some shared values in NLP, and Robert Dilts elicited and identified some shared values of the NLP Community during the Millennium Project. If you are interested in reading more about this, the results of his work can be found on his website.[1]

One belief we do all share is NLP works. We all have personal experience of this fact and I am sure we do all have

---

[1] http//:www.nlpu.com/millenR.htm.

many experiences we can relate and share. We can recall many occasions where NLP has made a positive difference to our lives and the lives of others.

I am in a really fortunate position, in that I do get to hear about other people's success with NLP on a regular basis. We share these stories through *Rapport*, and on our website, and it is my dream to have success stories on our website about every single subject where NLP has made a difference. This way, anyone searching for help with their particular issue will discover NLP is a viable option for them.

This will come as no surprise to us because we all know NLP works and it can make a huge difference to people's lives. So maybe it would be worth remembering our commonly held beliefs and values next time we find ourselves in discord with a fellow NLP practitioner.

As Virginia Satir said 'Feelings of worth can flourish only in an atmosphere where individual differences are appreciated, mistakes are tolerated, communication is open, and rules are flexible – the kind of atmosphere that is found in a nurturing family.'

...Chunking down

We are so lucky to have experience of a subject which is hugely diverse in its applications, because it means we can all find slightly different ways of applying our skills, which means overall there will be more people able to benefit from NLP.

I remember inwardly debating with myself which subject to take at university. If I had chosen biology, I had a vast choice of potential universities I could attend, because virtually every university in the UK offered a degree in biology. But what I really wanted to do was genetics, because this was the subject which really fascinated me...so at the time, my choice of UK universities was limited to only six (I'm showing my age now, as I'm sure there is a lot more choice for potential geneticists nowadays.). But because there were only six universities which offered genetics as a subject, you can be assured every budding geneticist immediately focused on those six universities and completely ignored the rest.

Like genetics, NLP is a specialised subject in itself, and has such a vast range of potential applications the opportunities are virtually limitless. There are NLP practitioners who specialise in using NLP for weight loss, for increasing confidence, for team building, for dyslexia, for relationships, for phobias, for managing ill health, for allergies, for improving communication skills, for enhancing performance and even for improving eyesight…and I am sure you can think of many others.

You are unique in recognising and understanding the practical applications of NLP when combined with your life experiences and skills in a certain way. It therefore follows you are best placed to apply your NLP skills in those areas you already understand and niche your services accordingly.

I met a teacher on an NLP training course and her passion was getting NLP into education. As a head teacher, she was very well placed to introduce NLP from the inside.

She had successfully done this in her own school, and because she had such recognisable success, she had been headhunted by the local authority and asked to do the same in a failing school within the same area. She applied the models which worked, and when I met her, she was starting to achieve some small steps towards success with the new school, and was working on a project to roll this out to other schools in her area.

There are many NLP trainers I know who have successfully combined their NLP skills with their existing experience and created something unique in their field.

An NLP Trainer friend of mine, Julie Inglis, has successfully combined her personal experiences with her NLP skills and runs courses in Hertfordshire for 'Managing Autistic Spectrum Conditions and ADHD using NLP'.

Hertfordshire County Council subsidise these courses, because they have the evidence to prove their key workers have a greater impact with the people in their care once they have some relevant NLP skills to include in their portfolio. They have measured this impact from a financial perspective and have proof the council is saving money on adult care now they are using NLP.

This means in Hertfordshire at least, parents, carers, social workers and other key staff have the opportunity to learn about NLP and how it can make a difference to their lives and the lives of those affected by Asperger's, Autism and ADHD.

Julie is driven by a passion which comes from personal understanding because her children have Asperger's. I have attended this course and I know what a difference it makes because my young son also has Asperger's. Thanks to the foresight of Hertfordshire County Council, there are now people throughout Hertfordshire who are also experiencing the difference NLP can make to their lives.

TIP

By applying your NLP to areas you already understand and niching your services, you automatically create some credibility within your targeted field. As one of my mentors, Bev James would say, 'generalists seek clients and clients seek specialists'.

Richard Churches is the Principal Consultant for the Centre for British Teachers (CfBT) Education Trust. Richard has been an Advanced Skills Teacher, as well as a manager in inner city secondary schools in London and an Ofsted Inspector. He has been a senior leader and advisor in many government led education initiatives. He is therefore well placed and experienced in the education field.

Richard combines this experience with his understanding of NLP and has been responsible for some very interesting and enlightening books and research papers, including *NLP for Teachers*,[2] which he co-authored with Roger Terry. He has been able to secure research funding for NLP in education and continues to work within the education sector to introduce the concepts of NLP into the education system.

Contrast this with a call we had a few years ago now, from a concerned dad. His 18-year-old daughter had recently been on a transformational weekend, and as a result, now wanted to leave university (where she had been for less than a term), and pursue her career as an NLP practitioner...she had been promised a fantastic deal whereby she would become an NLP trainer within three months and be earning vast amounts of money within a year.

This dad was a little sceptical and concerned about his daughter's intentions to become an NLP trainer earning a six figure salary in just one year, and I asked what she was studying at university, that she was so keen to give up. It turned out she was studying drama and acting, and by talking things through with this dad, he was able to find an acceptable compromise solution to propose to his daughter.

The compromise was his daughter could continue her university studies alongside her interest in NLP, because it could be quite possible for her to discover a niche of clients within the acting profession who would benefit from her skills...and it turned out the 'financial deal of a lifetime' she was being offered was not so great anyway.

By combining your skills with what you already know and understand, as well as raising your credibility as an NLP

---

[2] Churches, R. and Terry, R. *NLP for Teachers: how to be a highly effective teacher.* Carmarthen; Crown House Publishing 2007.

practitioner within your own field of expertise, you are also creating a solid foundation for your NLP business. Your target audience could be right there in front of you. After all, if you have benefitted from applying your NLP in your life, then so could your work colleagues, associates and clients.

My friend, Suzanne Henwood did just this, and once she had completed her NLP training, she started introducing NLP into the health sector. As a clinical radiographer and academic, she was able to do this because she could translate her NLP into terms which were more acceptable to a health professional, and bridge the language gap between the health service and NLP.

In fact, after my surgery, I did give my surgeon a copy of her book, *NLP and Coaching for Healthcare Professionals: developing expert practice* (co-authored with Jim Lister)[3] because I realised this was more likely to resonate with him and maybe strike a greater chord of understanding than some of the other great NLP books I know and love.

> **TIP**
>
> *NLP Professionals provide solutions – ask yourself what your niche could be and what problems would your niche solve?*

Once you have a clear idea about what area you could develop as your specific niche, you will find it much easier to create your business plan and identify your target market of clients. Then you will be able to devise your promotional and marketing materials so you are able to build rapport and communicate with your potential clients really effectively.

I do understand it is tempting to want to keep your options open rather than limit your stream of potential clients, so I would encourage you to think for a moment: when you need someone to fix the damage to your expensive Victorian oak flooring, you are likely to search for an oak flooring specialist, rather than a straight forward carpenter. Your Victorian oak

---

[3] Henwood, S. and Lister, J. *NLP and Coaching for Healthcare Professionals: developing expert practice.* Chichester; John Wiley & Sons, 2007.

flooring is valuable to you and you would prefer to hire a specialist to repair your damaged floor.

The same applies to NLP – it is quite a challenging subject to sell in the first place, so if you are promoting yourself as being able to fix all things to all people, how are your potential clients going to specifically understand how you can help them? Presumably, you would rather stand out in your particular area of expertise and attract those clients who really will benefit from your help.

I certainly messed up when I went charging full pelt into my new coaching business, joining the breakfast networking group without even making any real plans first – what type of coaching did I want to do? Who were my intended clients? Where would I be most likely to find these clients?

Once I stepped back and thought about my actions, and my longer term plans, in hindsight, I realised I was never likely to find my clients at a breakfast business networking group, because my dream was to join with other NLP practitioners so we could collectively make a bigger difference. I wasn't likely to find too many of them networking in the golf club at 7 a.m. every week.

What had happened to me in this situation was I had become very motivated whilst in the safe environment of the coaching weekend, which had really opened my eyes to the wealth of new possibilities which were open to me. I was a bit like the child in the sweetie shop, wanting some of everything...now... without considering the consequences and the alternative ways of getting to sample all the sweets in the shop.

We do need to have a clear outcome and plan for what we do want to achieve, so we do have something to focus on and keep us on the right track, especially when we do get out into the real world.

TIP

To help you identify your niche, identify those people you enjoy working with most – could they become your niche market?

It is the differences in our approach, in our application and in the way we have been taught which contribute so much to the continual evolution of NLP. We are privileged to be involved with a relatively new subject and its flexibility means we are always refining, improving and discovering new ways of applying the things we have learned and understood from our own NLP training.

NLP itself was derived from modelling various therapies and approaches, and NLP has continued to evolve and contribute to other related subjects such as Clean Language and New Code NLP.

These differences are healthy and contribute to the continual evolution of products and services from which we can all benefit.

Take Mr Dyson, for example. Vacuum cleaners had already been around for a very long time – in one form or another our mothers and grandmothers had used them, and over the years, they had evolved (and diversified) into either a cylinder or upright model. These types of vacuum cleaners had been around for many decades and apart from some cosmetic enhancements, had changed very little. We all accepted and used these machines and probably thought no more about it.

Then Dyson came along and completely revolutionised the world of the vacuum cleaner – he managed to find even better ways of cleaning which were completely different to anything which had gone before. He developed a whole new range of products using his revolutionary new technology and transformed the world of vacuum cleaners ... simply by being a bit different.

NLP is a wonderful subject for keeping us on our toes and offers us the opportunity to be creative and develop further applications and uses. As another challenge arises in our world, it is fairly certain someone will work out how NLP can be applied to this challenge.

I see NLP as a bit like giving a child a cardboard box. If you watch a child playing with a cardboard box, their natural curiosity and imagination knows no boundaries. When we moved house, my son created a whole new world of possibilities. The packing boxes were transformed into robots and houses and space ships and trucks and beds. They were chopped up and stuck together and coloured and decorated...they provided hours of endless fun and creativity and imagination and possibilities in the mind of a young child.

Isn't this exactly what NLP gives us – opportunities, possibilities and the chance to be creative and discover new resources? It is this curiosity and creativity and different ways of thinking which contribute to the development of NLP. One person looks at the cardboard box and sees a spaceship...and another sees a submarine or a robot. All are right because NLP, like a cardboard box, has at least 101 potential uses.

TIP

Explaining what you do is much easier when you have a niche. Try completing the sentence, 'I help people to...'

As I mentioned, one of the models we sometimes seem to adopt in the NLP community is division. There are some infamous splits within the NLP community, the most widely recognised being Richard Bandler and John Grinder, the two co-founders of NLP.

I believe it is time to acknowledge these divisions, recognise the benefits...and move on. It is possible to do this – the Russians did it, even if it did mean dividing themselves into many small and more manageable, but different countries. They do still share the same space, it's just mapped out differently now.

It is common knowledge Bandler and Grinder publicly disagreed and fell out over NLP. This is OK, whatever happened is between Richard and John, and none of us, as observers, will ever know everything which really went on...as long as we remember 'the map is not the territory' and apply this to their situation as well.

We do know despite their later differences, they co-created something which we all find empowering and beneficial. They created it, and collectively, ever since they shared their ideas back in the 1970s, we have all played a part in the continued development and evolution of NLP.

Bandler and Grinder have gone their separate ways, and they have each developed new ideas based on NLP for themselves. Others have come together since then, developed ideas and publicly split as well. It seems some of the early movers and shakers in NLP have inadvertently created some less than useful models which often divide the community.

I must admit, I do wonder sometimes, how this could have happened, given the presuppositions of NLP – principles which form the foundation of NLP and have been modelled from key people who consistently produce superb results, as well as from systems theory and natural laws.

We are taught these are useful beliefs to adopt, and can help us to make some sense of the world. In which case, perhaps we do need to assume at the time, these divisions occurred because behind every behaviour is a positive intention. The one presupposition which could usefully be applied now is 'having respect for another person's model of the world'.

Some of those early co-creators of NLP may choose to never speak to each other again – the point is, does it really affect us? NLP has moved on since then and we can choose to view NLP as the whole in which we all play a part. This means we all have a collective say in how NLP moves forward from now on.

We can all choose to decide division within the community may have a positive intention for the few people who follow this model (they seem to have many impassioned followers), but it does have a detrimental effect on NLP as a whole and can cause massive confusion for the public...who then walk away and try something else instead, because they have no idea who they should train with and what lineage is best.

So how about we collectively decide to be extremely grateful to John and Richard for what they co-created, we now choose to model the best parts of NLP, and we choose to leave behind the divisions between lineages, respect each other's model of the world, acknowledge all these lineages have a part to play in the evolution of NLP...and move towards a more united NLP community which accepts the differences within it, celebrates the successes and similarities and starts to focus outwards towards the society in which we want to make a difference.

Summary

By chunking up and recognising all NLP Professionals have something to offer to the NLP Profession, you will recognise the diversity in NLP is about niching your services, not who you trained with... and by niching your services and becoming an expert in your particular NLP area of expertise, you will attract those clients seeking a specialist to help them address a particular issue. Overall, you will be contributing to NLP becoming more widely recognised as a credible solution for helping with lots of specific issues.

Celebrate your differences

CHAPTER SIX

Working Collaboratively

'The whole is more than the sum of its parts.'

Aristotle, philosopher (384–322BC)

All NLP practitioners currently run 'small businesses', when using the UK definition of a small company.[1] They stand proudly and independently, and sometimes view any form of collaboration with a fellow NLP practitioner as 'fraternising with the enemy'.

NLP Professionals realise the power of working collaboratively and pooling resources on occasions, so collectively we can get NLP out there into the public arena and make sure we are noticed.

NLP Professionals can apply the 'Daffodil Principle' to their business and recognise the 'power of the people', especially when it comes to working towards recognition of NLP as an accepted profession and with regard to any potential regulation or legislation.

I'd like to sow a few seeds and suggest some reframes which could make a difference to the way you view your business, and perhaps even NLP as a whole.

---

[1] Currently a small company is defined as having:
   ▼ an annual turnover of £5.6 million or less;
   ▼ total fixed and current assets on its balance sheet of £2.8 million or less; and
   ▼ 50 employees or less.

Think for a moment, of Aristotle's famous quote. He made this observation a few thousand years ago, and maybe it still holds true today? The whole concept of coalition is to maintain your own identity whilst collaborating with others.

NLP is still a fledgling and evolving profession, so is still relatively unknown compared to some other, more established practices. Market research which we commissioned indicated 79% of people questioned had no knowledge or understanding of what the acronym NLP stood for.[2]

This in itself was a fairly niche poll, so in reality, there may be even more people across the UK who have never heard of NLP. So there is still plenty of work to be done in getting NLP noticed out there.

Remember your basic chemistry lessons from school days. At a young age, when I was first introduced to the wonderful world of chemical reactions, I remember being absolutely fascinated by the equation

You will remember this means when hydrogen and oxygen are combined, they make water. Isn't this an amazing act of nature (or science) which can take two gases, and effectively combines them to create water, an essential part of our lives without which none of us could survive. On their own, neither hydrogen nor oxygen can even be seen, yet when they team up together, they create something completely different and certainly something bigger and more noticeable than either of them when taken in isolation.

[2] Market research poll of 1,000 individuals undertaken at Farnborough Air Show, Hampshire, UK.

There are many examples of successful partnerships outside the chemical world. I know I am showing my age, but do you recall Morecombe and Wise, the comedy duo who combined their skills, timing and talent to become one of the most famous and successful comedy acts ever in the UK? In fact, even if you are younger than me, you will probably have come across them because their Christmas specials are still repeated year after year and feature in every 'best of' programme ever made.

I'm not for one moment suggesting you go out tomorrow and look for an NLP partner with whom you can join forces and become the biggest double act since Morecombe and Wise. I am, for now, inviting you to chunk up around the whole concept of the 'whole being greater than the sum of its parts', and start to think about NLP being the 'whole'. Then we will become the parts which could combine to create something bigger and more noticeable like the NLP Profession.

This is the concept behind my Daffodil Principle: imagine, for a moment, a daffodil. One daffodil is unique, individual and beautiful when captured in solitude, where its beauty can be focused upon and magnified; notice the colour combinations and perfect tonality between the trumpet of the daffodil and its petals; notice how it stands in magnificent splendour, tall, upright and proud.

Now think about a whole field containing 50,000 daffodils, all standing tall and proud, their brilliant yellow petals catching the spring sunshine, and a ripple of movement as the slight breeze catches them. Collectively they form a sea of bright yellow which seems to stretch as far as the eye can see – and for a moment, the impact of this magnificent yellow ocean completely takes your breath away.

To get NLP noticed and making an impact in society, we do need to combine our individual strengths, and pull together our unique talents so NLP creates the same impact as the sea of daffodils.

This works well for daffodils, but does it work with people?

NLP was originally modelled on individuals rather than teams or groups, so I think there is a tendency, on occasions, for us to believe we can do it on our own. Sometimes, however omnipotent we would like to think we are, there is great value in working together to get NLP noticed, so we can collectively start to make a bigger difference.

A perfect example of this is those big charity events which now take place regularly and raise millions of pounds in one day for Children in Need or Comic Relief. People from all over the UK pull together and combine their resources to make these events happen.

Celebrities set an example (and use their celebrity status) to pull in the money for these worthy causes and engage with us all, encouraging us all to do our bit...and we see the results of this as the totals raised get bigger every year. It is fun, it is enjoyable, and we get a sense of team spirit and satisfaction from being part of something bigger and playing a small part in contributing to the £102 million raised,[3] which really will make a difference to many people.

How could we apply this to NLP? Well, how about combining our resources, sharing our skills and our successes and doing our bit to ensure NLP gets out there and is noticed?

If you need reminding about the potential benefits of collaboration, think, for a moment, of a rainbow. The sun and rain, when they do combine their resources, create a magnificent array of colours in a rainbow...which most people do tend to notice.

Closer to home, the International NLP Research Conference is an example of collaboration between individuals to put on something of benefit for the whole NLP community. The first International NLP Research Conference, which was held

---

[3] http://www.comicrelief.com/news/2011-05/record-breaking-%C2%A3102-million-total.

at the University of Surrey in July 2008, was born out of a conversation which grew after Paul Tosey, Charles Faulkner and I were having a coffee in Canary Wharf. Between us, we recruited other team players (the committee) and created the whole conference and subsequent journal, *Current Research in NLP.*

I do think our team collaboration and understanding of the bigger picture impact carried us through and gave us the driving force to ensure our success. We were motivated by each other along the way and we did all have a sense what we were creating would be significant and positively beneficial for NLP as a whole.

The concept of sharing and collaboration is a challenging model to adopt sometimes, especially in the field of NLP, where more divisive models have been used in the past. This is changing and I believe the future of NLP lies in encouraging a more collaborative approach.

I attended 'Passion in Action' a few years ago, an NLP workshop specifically run to support social enterprises and community projects. I was listening to Judith DeLozier and Judith Lowe explain about the concept of sharing. It was important and significant for us all to understand, at the time, sharing ideas was a good thing to do and was different to sharing money. Their simple explanation went as follows:

> *'If I give you a pound and you give me a pound, then we each walk away with a pound. If I share my idea with you and you share your idea with me, then we each walk away with two ideas...which could then become three or more, as we use those ideas to generate others'.*

Remember, someone else understanding or knowing about NLP does not affect your understanding and knowledge of NLP. Surgeons, thankfully, share their skills and knowledge and discoveries about new and better operating techniques, so the whole of medicine, and therefore the patients, benefit from these enhancements.

In the same way, all those people who contributed to the NLP research conference were happy to share their research with others, so this information could be more widely understood and appreciated. Each presenter delivered their research piece to their audience ... and at the moment, having only recently launched the resulting NLP research journal, we can only guess what knock on effect this additional knowledge and sharing of information could have.

We have all experienced this momentum, the surge of energy which comes from being part of a group of like minded people. We know there is power in numbers, because we have probably all witnessed situations where the energy of a group takes us forward and possibly gives us enough confidence to do something we would not necessarily have done if we were on our own. Tony Robbins' firewalk springs to mind and is modelled by many others – it perfectly models collaboration and teamwork in order to create greater confidence and motivation in the individuals within the team.

TIP

Join a local Practice Group...and if there isn't one locally, then collaborate with other local NLP professionals and set one up.

I do know of some NLP practitioners who do form associate groups with their colleagues because this does create a sense of confidence for potential clients – the perception there is something bigger rather than just one person does seem to make a difference to a client, even if they only deal with you.

I remember, when looking for a new GP because we had recently moved house, I searched for GP practices which were partnerships rather than sole practitioners. My reason was I wanted a choice of doctors within the practice and I felt strongly a partnership had a better support structure in place for me and my family. Maybe it is simply a case of there being safety in numbers.

If I can digress into the retail world for a moment, think about Bicester Village. It is probably one of the most well known Outlet Retail Parks in the UK, and people travel from all over the UK to visit it. Yet Bicester Village is simply a very successful combination of small shops which have combined their designer names and individual reputations to create a centre which attracts millions of visitors every year (and who all seem to visit the same day I choose to go.).

Very few people had heard of the little town of Bicester before 'Bicester Village' opened, and I do know of the incredible impact this collaborative venture has had, because it is the area in which I grew up.

For most NLP practitioners, there is a great benefit to creating a network of contacts, especially because many of us do work in isolation. Not only do we benefit from sharing time and resources with colleagues, we also have the opportunity to create a contact list of other NLP practitioners in our area. Imagine how useful this could be the next time you may need a bit of extra help with your business.

Eve Menezes Cunningham, one of our *Rapport* journalists, wrote a wonderful article recently about 'how being extra helpful can be good for business'. She explained how valuable it could be to help out a potential client by referring them on to someone else if there is some reason you cannot help them at this time, rather than just saying 'no'. Some people tend to remember acts of kindness and those times when someone has gone the extra mile, and it can reap benefits in the long run.

I do remember a few years ago, being so busy with my accounts work I recommended a potential client to another accountant, as I felt I could not give them the service they deserved at the time. Later the same year, when I was not quite so busy, the same accountant recommended me to a potential client, who turned out to be a hugely enjoyable and lucrative client to work with.

Martin Weaver, one of our members, has a great network of contacts which he has created, and, as a psychotherapist, he has a brilliant arrangement with some of his business contacts whereby they cross refer, so he takes on those clients who require a more psychotherapeutic approach. His business colleagues take on some of those clients who require a more straight forward NLP/coaching model.

So having a network of contacts can reap rewards, even if they are in the same field in which you already work.

TIP

Get together with local NLP Professionals and consider working together to promote your services. It is better to run one combined workshop than cancel two smaller ones because the numbers were not sufficient.

At this point, I would like to reiterate the difference between rivalry and competition:

'Competition', as defined by the Collins dictionary, is 'a contest in which a winner is selected from among two or more entrants'.

A 'rival', as defined by the same dictionary, is 'a person or thing that is considered the equal of another'.

So, if we were to compete with each other for business, there is an inference there will be winners and losers, and in a way this is true – only one person can win a particular piece of work.

So let's reframe for a moment and imagine what could happen if our attitude was more about having rivals than having competition. We could then enjoy a healthy rivalry with our colleagues in the field of NLP, rather than feeling the need to compete with them at every level and be the winner.

Think of sport, for example, where week in, week out, on various pitches, fields, arenas and tracks around the world, sports rivals compete to be the best in their chosen sport. There are clear winners, and losers, and the rivalry is fierce both between the competitors and between their rival supporters. But despite this rivalry and competition on the field, there is usually a healthy respect between players and athletes, both on and off the field.

Contrast this approach with the one taken by politicians during an election. During an election campaign, they are competing with each other to win a seat and represent their party, and their constituents in parliament. Their primary objective is to win the seat so their party becomes the one to lead the country.

However, there seems to be no love lost between candidates, and they seem to spend the majority of their time telling us how bad their opposition is, rather than informing us about how good they will be. If they can use words to effectively denigrate and destroy their opposition, they will do.

Does this work? I know I personally find this approach distasteful and unhelpful – I would prefer to see politicians showing a modicum of respect for their rivals. After all, their models of the world may differ, but at the end of the day, all the candidates presumably share some similar reasons for wanting to succeed.

We have now experienced a coalition government and whilst not all elements always run smoothly, I wonder if there are some elements of successful coalitions which could be modelled so individual NLP Professionals could retain their own identity whilst collaborating to promote NLP.

Aside from politics, I can think of one or two other examples where this idea of coalition or collaboration does work well. What about Formula 1 racing, where all the drivers compete for an individual championship, at the same time as representing their team, who have an eye on the constructors' championship.

What about the TV programme, *The Apprentice*? Wouldn't it be true to say whilst all the contestants are competing for one prize, they initially stand the best chance of winning the prize by working as a team, so they can win the challenge every week.

I do think sometimes, like the contestants on *The Apprentice*, the field of NLP is quite inward looking and tends to focus in on the NLP community rather than outwards at the general public. Remember the research – at least 79% of the public have never heard of NLP...so if they haven't even heard of it, then it probably isn't going to be within their range of options when they are facing a particular challenge.

So what could happen, if we started working together from the point of view NLP needs to be noticed and recognised as a viable option first? Let's future pace and imagine, just for a moment, we have reached the stage where everyone in the UK now knows NLP is a credible solution for their particular problem...

Let's assume your ideal business model is to be seeing two clients a day, i.e. 10 clients a week, and you only take four weeks' holiday every year. Let's also assume the average client likes to have the equivalent of 10 NLP coaching sessions. Now let's be generous and assume even though the whole UK population (currently 60 million, and rising) knows about NLP, only half of them want to hire an NLP Professional for 10 sessions.

So how long would it take you, on your own, to coach half the UK population? It would take you 625,000 years to coach half the UK population (i.e. 30,000,000 people x 10 sessions ÷ [48 weeks x 10 clients per week] = 625,000 years).

What if you are a trainer? Perhaps your ideal business model is to run four NLP training courses a year, with 250 people on each course (you may as well think big). It would take you a mere 30,000 years to train half the population (i.e. 30,000,000 people ÷ [250 per course x 4 per year] = 30,000 years)...and this is only to Practitioner level.

Now, unless you have discovered the secret to eternal life, I suspect this isn't going to happen. So, if we really do believe NLP can make a difference then perhaps we do need to work together to get NLP known about, and then we can all take a share in the increased demand for our services.

At least this way, by acknowledging there is plenty of potential business to go around, we could collectively coach half the UK population a little more quickly, because I don't want to wait 625,000 years before the social impact of NLP really does start making a difference to society.

Even with this abundance reframe, NLP practitioners may still question why would we want to work together? Sometimes, greater things can be achieved as a team.

Think about the 'Team GB' relay team who represent us in the Olympics. Our runners, as individuals, do not even reach the final of the 100 metres. But as a team, we can, and do win medals in the 100 metres relay finals because somehow, whatever the four runners put together as a team creates something which is more powerful and successful than each of them as individual runners.

Our Team GB relay runners certainly demonstrate the principle behind one of my favourite quotes by Mattie Stepanek (American poet, 1990–2004):

'Unity is strength... when there is teamwork and collaboration wonderful things can be achieved.'

Let's imagine, for a moment, there was a 'Team NLP', made up of every person who has ever invested in NLP and brought into the principle of the NLP Profession. So what great things could Team NLP achieve? What parts of the model could we adopt in order to make Team NLP succeed, and in the process, ensure every individual within Team NLP also enjoys success?

For a start, one of the things Team NLP would do is work as a team – just like in the relay, personal differences and squabbles are left behind once the race starts and everyone does work as a team when it counts. There may be squabbles along the way – golly, my brother and I used to fight like cat and dog when we were children. But when he got knocked out at school one day (not by me, I hasten to add), and was rushed to hospital, all those squabbles, disagreements and arguments were forgotten and we really pulled together as a family to make sure he was OK.

If we really need convincing about the value of teamwork, just remember how communities pull together, both in times of adversity, and also to achieve great things. This is often drawn to our attention when there is some sort of disaster, such as an earthquake or hurricane – we experienced this camaraderie for ourselves in 1980, when we were having our family holiday in Barbados, which was rather dramatically interrupted by the arrival of Hurricane Allen.

We didn't know anyone in the area, and yet everyone worked together to clear roads and ensure everyone in the community had adequate shelter...but they went further than this. They all helped each other rebuild their houses, their businesses and their schools and their communities – it really was 'one for all and all for one'.

Team NLP could model this camaraderie and team spirit to elevate NLP to the next level.

Think about a large corporation for a moment...one which employs thousands of people and has many different departments. It's a fairly safe bet that on occasions, there is in house squabbling between departments, and there will be times when 'Sales' disagrees with 'Marketing', 'Finance' have an argument with 'Admin' and everyone falls out with 'HR'.

Whatever the internal disagreements, you can be fairly certain as far as the public face of the company is concerned, it presents a united front where everything appears to be harmonious and runs smoothly. The public front of the company is usually what the public will be buying into, so it is important it looks good, from the outside at least.

We all recognise more damage is done to any one of the political parties when they 'wash their dirty linen in public', as my grandma used to say. Even if it does amuse us as curious observers, it never seems to do a great deal for their popularity rating.

The same applies to NLP as a profession. As NLP Professionals, we could do our bit to chunk up and ensure NLP, as a whole, is recognised by the public as a viable alternative, at which point we can each step up as individuals and offer to play our part.

Working collaboratively does have an effect at every level. Life is about teamwork and I would suggest collaboration ultimately plays a part in every success. So it is really important to recognise and nurture the teams which have a role in your life, including your:

▼ *Inner team.*

▼ *Role with clients.*

▼ *Role within the NLP profession.*

Your inner team

The Team we sometimes overlook when thinking about teamwork is our inner team – all those things which play a part in our own physical, mental emotional and spiritual well being. There are the obvious ways of nurturing our own inner team – ensuring we eat a healthy diet; addressing physical issues like aches and pains; ensuring we get sufficient rest and treating our bodies with care; making sure we take downtime for relaxation and mental rejuvenation and creating regular time out for ourselves.

John Seymour introduces the concept of the 'Seven Practices of Transformational NLP', which he identified after noticing some of his NLP students seemed to get far greater benefit out of their NLP than others. He acknowledges there is a difference between inter-personal skills, i.e. communication between people, and intra-personal skills, i.e. communication within a person, and suggests it is the intra-personal skills which are the essential ones for personal development and transformational learning.

TIP

Read John Seymour's article in **Rapport** *issue 15, Spring 2009 or read online at http://www.anlp.org/files/the-7-practices-of-transformational-nlp_37_179.pdf.*

We do know the principles of putting ourselves first on occasions, and at least remembering we are part of the equation. I have been reminded, more than once, of the life jacket principle – if you are caught on the sinking ship, it is very important to put a life jacket on yourself first, because this way, you are then in a much better position to be able to help your family, or the others around you. After all, you are not likely to be much help to them if you end up sinking first.

The trick is then getting the right balance between looking after ourselves and looking after others...and that's another story.

Your role with clients

The teamwork we are possibly most familiar with is the team we create with our clients as we coach and support them to achieve their intended outcomes. No doubt we can all recollect occasions when we have really experienced this sense of teamwork when working with a client, or with our own coach.

I am privileged to be experiencing this teamwork right now, as Mindy Gibbins-Klein coaches me to realise my dream of writing a book. Last year, writing a book was something I had always aspired to, but it was something others did and was never going to be possible for me.

And then I read Mindy's book, *24 Carat BOLD*,[4] and was so inspired I contacted her and asked what I had to do next... and here I am. And whilst I have discovered my own inner resources and called upon them to get me to this place, it would probably have taken me another lifetime or two to find them and get here on my own. Maybe I was looking for the needle in the haystack, and then Mindy lent me the metal detector.

We do witness this sort of teamwork all the time and acknowledge sometimes it does take someone else to bring out the best in us. Gok Wan is a wonderful example of this, and I love sharing the transformational journeys he takes with his clients on the TV programme, *How to Look Good Naked*.

His manner can sometimes be a little surprising and certainly a little irreverent (that's TV entertainment for you, I guess), and yet every week, he succeeds in guiding a woman to look at herself in a completely new light. Unlike some other makeover TV shows, he doesn't bring in the plastic surgeons and dentists and designer gowns to help with the makeover. He just takes his client on a joyous journey of self discovery, and shows her how to make the best of herself with what she already has...talk about helping us to discover the hidden resources we all have within us.

---

[4] Gibbins-Klein, M. *24 Carat BOLD: Claim Your Position as the Top Expert in Your Field.* Penryn; Ecademy Press, 2009.

Your role within the NLP profession

So what exactly is teamwork in the field? Am I talking about the team created between the shepherd, his sheepdog and the flock of sheep, as they successfully move smoothly seamlessly from one end of the field to a pen at the other end? Not quite, although this does work as an example of teamwork.

There are many professional fields, other than those which readily spring to mind. Actors form part of a profession, and even when one actor wins an Oscar, there is a whole team of people they usually thank for helping them get as far as the winner's podium.

Let's face it, for starters, they usually have to have starred in a film in order to be noticed and nominated for an Oscar. And we all know, from the rolling credits at the end of every film, just how many hundreds of people play a part in getting this actor onto our cinema screen.

And what about our own professional field, i.e. the field of NLP. Remember Team NLP? We all belong to Team NLP by virtue of the fact we have had training in NLP. Some of us may be more active team players than others and we all have a part to play in developing and nurturing and protecting the NLP profession.

This is where the professional bodies and/or trade associations come in. Most professions do have a professional body (or two) – solicitors have the Law Society, doctors have the British Medical Association (BMA) and accountants successfully operate with a framework of more than one professional body, such as the Institute of Chartered Accountants, the Chartered Institute of Management Accountants and the Association of Chartered Certified Accountants.

The main benefit of the professional bodies and trade associations is the added value they give to the profession as a whole. They can act as the collective voice on behalf of their members and ensure members are represented when it matters, i.e. in the regulation debate, with standards setting and with accreditation.

ANLP belongs to the Federation of Small Businesses (FSB) and Social Enterprises East of England (SEEE). We do get some benefits of membership, should we choose to take them, such as free business banking, a credit card and a free legal helpline.

What has more value for us, however, is representation and a say when things happen which could affect small businesses or social enterprises. I always fill out the surveys which come from both the FSB and SEEE, because this is our way of having a voice, and lending our membership to the collective voice of small businesses and social enterprises.

For example, the FSB stand a much greater chance of successfully lobbying parliament about issues affecting small businesses if they can say they surveyed their members and out of 300,000 responses, 87% of small businesses are concerned about the effect of increasing petrol prices or have been adversely affected by the change in employment law.

As one small business in the UK, I'm sure I would have to write an awful lot of letters to my MP and various cabinet ministers to have the same collective impact as the FSB...and I know parliament would talk to the FSB to seek their opinion and the opinion of their members. The government would need a pretty huge table if they were to consider inviting me and every other small business in the UK (which make up 95% of British businesses) to a round table discussion about the effects of their latest proposed business legislation.

Tip: Join some of the social NLP Groups on LinkedIn, and start contributing to the group dynamic. These groups include the Association for NLP group (http://www.linkedin. com/groups?gid=2464853&trk=hb_side_g) and the NLP Research Conference group (http://www.linkedin.com/ groups?gid=3117953&trk=hb_side_g).

We could also acknowledge the benefits of building strategic alliances, partnering with others for specific purposes or projects. We have many Strategic Alliances within ANLP and enjoy building teams, partnerships and relationships in order to create something of value for others.

We work with the universities and a committee of volunteers to put together the NLP research conference; we engage with the NLP community to report successes and share applications of NLP through *Rapport*; we introduce like minded people within the community so they can share resources and work collaboratively to support and develop their ideas for a particular sector of society. *Acuity*, the research journal, the social media groups and practice groups are all examples to remind us, and our potential clients, there is an emerging professional field for NLP.

We are simply modelling strategic alliances which happen successfully on a wider scale. Think about the North Atlantic Treaty Organisation (NATO), the World Health Organisation (WHO) and the United Nations (UN).

I am sure you can think of models which would work within the NLP community. Wouldn't it be fun to chunk up and apply some NLP to the community, rather than always focusing on the individuals within it.

How about some Time Line work, so any negative feelings from the past can be acknowledged and the useful learnings taken from those past events and applied now.

What about some parts integration work to discover the positive intention behind the divisions and heal the conflicts of the past?

How about we all adopt the presuppositions of NLP and apply these to the community as well as to ourselves?

Ooooohhh, the possibilities are endless, and the great thing is, we already know about them. So collectively, it could be quite simple to make these things happen.

Summary

By reframing things as an NLP Professional, and starting to view NLP as the team to which we all belong, the reasons for collaborating and working with others become more apparent.

By working collaboratively, we can collectively take responsibility for raising the profile of NLP, getting it more widely accepted as a profession and pool our resources so NLP is noticed for the right reasons.

Work collaboratively

CHAPTER SEVEN

Raising Awareness of NLP

'The first step toward change is awareness.
The second step is acceptance.'

Nathaniel Branden, psychotherapist (1930–)

Even with the efforts of individual practitioners, training schools and organisations like ANLP, NLP is still not widely recognised as a credible solution to many of life's challenges.

There are many reasons for this already covered in previous chapters, and these cumulate in a lack of understanding about what NLP is and how it can help an individual.

NLP Professionals recognise the need to raise awareness of NLP by effective marketing and they embrace every opportunity to raise the profile of NLP. NLP Professionals understand by raising the profile of NLP, they are ultimately increasing demand for their services as an NLP Professional. NLP Professionals allocate a budget for marketing and realise it is an essential part of their overall business strategy.

Paul Tosey and Jane Mathison identified in their book, *Neuro-Linguistic Programming: a critical appreciation for managers and developers,*[1] NLP is at a crossroads and has so far failed to become accepted as a mainstream practice. They cite the factional nature as being one of the issues which has

---

[1] Tosey, P. and Mathison, J. *Neuro-Linguistic programming: a critical appreciation for managers and developers.* Basingstoke; Palgrave Macmillan, 2009.

contributed to this failure, and perhaps it is true we don't always have the best role models in NLP.

So apart from recognising we could all take on board our own presuppositions and pay more attention to respecting other people's model of the world, where does this leave us now? The past is the past, and we are where we are now. We, as Practitioners of NLP, collectively hold the power to shape our own future and the future of our field.

It could be helpful to understand more about the bigger picture around how people make their decisions. This information could be used to identify ways in which we could work together to encourage more people to choose NLP as the natural solution to their particular problem, rather than alternatives such as cognitive behavioural therapy (CBT).

At ANLP, we hear the voices of the public on a daily basis and they talk to us about their perceptions of NLP as a profession because we are impartial and independent.

Since we are not actually offering our services to them as a practitioner or as a trainer, the public also talk to us about their challenges when looking for an NLP professional, and the issues they face when they want to make a decision about getting some help for their particular issue.

I have consolidated some of these voices to benefit us as a community because the main benefit from generating more interest in NLP would be a bigger pool of potential clients for you.

I am keen to share this information with you because like you, I want you to be successful as NLP Professionals. After all, we, as the NLP Community, are only going to make a big difference to society if we all recognise, value and accept our own important and individual contribution to the field of NLP.

There are some key areas into which I have grouped these observations around how the public make their decisions and choose NLP.

As a Profession, I would suggest we all have a part to play in:

▼ Ensuring NLP is the *one of the natural solutions chosen by the public when they have a problem.*

▼ *Changing the public perception of NLP so they find it easier to make this choice.*

▼ *Appreciating the importance of reputation.*

Before we look at these points in detail, it might be useful to remind ourselves how people make decisions? I have already talked about the concept of NLP Professionals offering solutions to specific problems and this pattern does emerge in the bigger picture concept of decision making (rather than the detail of a decision making strategy), and for now, let's call this the 'Decision Tree'.

Decision Tree

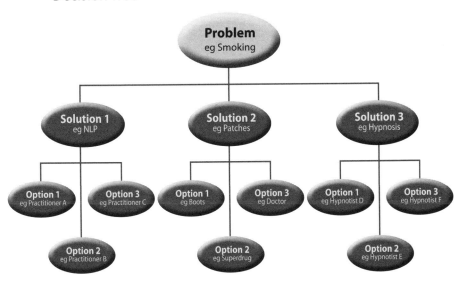

The Decision Tree starts with a problem or question which a member of the public needs to address. I think it would be easier to use an example to illustrate this, so the one I am going to use is smoking. The problem is this person...let's call him Fred... smokes and he wants to stop smoking (not the best phrase from an NLP perspective, but one which is universally recognised).

So, Fred has decided he wants to stop smoking and the first thing he would like to do is identify all the potential solutions or aids which could be useful in helping him. Let's assume he has already decided whilst he could go cold turkey, he's not confident he can do this on his own and he wants some additional support along the way.

Fred now has a number of options to consider...does he use nicotine patches, hypnosis or NLP – in fact it turns out there are many different solutions available which Fred can choose including counselling, CBT, emotional freedom technique (EFT) and homeopathy to help him stop smoking...so how does he decide which one to choose?

Fred is likely to be attracted to the option which captures his attention most powerfully – by the beacon which is shining brightest, the voice which is singing the sweetest song, or the emotion which tugs him most strongly.

And Fred will also rely upon the signposts which are out there, guiding him in one direction or another. These guides could influence him by pointing him in a particular direction and helping him to make a decision about whether to choose patches, or hypnosis or NLP. These guides, or facilitators are external influences and will include the internet, the NHS and the relevant associations or representative bodies.

Once Fred has decided on which particular path to take, he will then choose the specific solution to get him there. So, if he decides to use nicotine patches to help him quit smoking, then he will decide whether to get these from his GP, or Boots, or Superdrug, or his local independent chemist.

And if he chooses NLP, he will then choose the Practitioner who is most likely to satisfy his particular requirements. And at this stage, he will still be attracted by the beacon which is shining brightest, the voice which is singing the sweetest song, or the emotion which tugs him most strongly – but this time it will be on a more specific level.

There are occasions when the Decision Tree does work the other way round, and someone comes across a practitioner who is able to help with their challenge, only to discover afterwards NLP was the name of the tool being used. And this is absolutely fine, both ways of attracting a potential client work well and can be effective.

TIP

Use the Decision Tree model to help define your niche and define your own shining beacon of light.

However, if we were to harness this understanding of the bigger picture Decision Tree, and use this understanding alongside our existing individual marketing strategies, we could leverage things in favour of NLP.

So what effect does this Decision Tree have in ensuring NLP is one of the natural solutions chosen by the public when they have a problem? What does this have to do with changing the public perception of NLP so they know how to make a more informed choice more easily? And what is your personal role in all this?

To go back to my original comments about us all having a part to play...

Ensuring NLP is one of *the* natural solutions chosen by the public when they have a problem

It seems one of the challenges we face as an NLP community is the brightness of our light, the sweetness of our voice and the strength of our emotional tug...in other words, our power to attract...and if people do not even see NLP as an option for dealing with their particular problem, then NLP will not be their natural solution.

We have already established there is an incredibly low awareness about NLP. If less than 20% of the UK population have even heard of NLP, it's hardly surprising NLP is not always considered the first choice for someone like Fred who wants to quit smoking. Our beacon is not shining brightly enough.

My personal view is I see the NLP community as being a bit like a secret garden – we have a vast array of wonderful things to offer and between us we cover every single element you could possibly want in a garden – we have bountiful vegetable patches, beautiful rose gardens, practical areas for BBQing, areas where we can simply sit and enjoy, fun areas for playing and areas for being curious, a nursery garden for baby plants and even test beds for creating new species or improving the viability of existing species.

Yet most of this is well hidden, just like a secret garden, because, as a community, we have not yet succeeded in working together to present this beautiful, if secret garden to the public in a way which they can then enjoy it and benefit from it.

As sometimes NLP has had a bad press, what weakens the NLP message even further, and keeps it a well kept secret, is when NLP Professionals are using NLP, but calling it something else to avoid any negative reactions. So they are achieving success using NLP, and this success is not being attributed to NLP.

As a community of like minded people, we already understand the benefits of NLP because we have directly experienced them. I'm pretty certain we would be doing something else if we hadn't experienced some positive results from using NLP ourselves, so we already know what are talking about.

However we do not always communicate the benefits of NLP in a way which makes it easier for the public to understand how NLP could be the solution to their issue.

As I have mentioned previously, one of the keys to successfully promoting NLP is to use examples where your clients have experienced success using NLP to deal with a particular challenge, issue or problem.

These do need to be communicated in a way which is easily understood. These success stories, case studies or testimonials can be written in such a way someone facing a similar challenge could empathise and understand how NLP was able to help with overcoming the issue.

Most importantly, these stories need to focus on how NLP has made a practical and understandable difference to someone's life. Think about what your potential client will be able to empathise with and understand, rather than what you want to tell them.

If you were, for a moment, to step into the shoes of a member of the public, considering NLP as a possible solution to your particular issue (let's just say you want to stop smoking), which of these two statements would be more appealing to you?

A   *My name is George. I am an INPLTA ITA ABNLP SNLP NLPU NLP Practitioner based in Kent. I have trained all over the world with Richard Bandler, Wyatt Woodsmall, Robert Dilts, John Grinder and Tad James. I specialise in helping people stop smoking and I have been very successful in this area.*

B   *I was smoking 40 a day. I had tried all sorts of things to help
me stop smoking and nothing seemed to work. Before I went
to see George, an NLP Practitioner, I would get short of
breath and I could no longer run around the park with my
kids. Smoking was ruining my life. As a result of the
strategies taught to me by George, I have now chosen to quit
smoking and have not had a cigarette for over six months
now – I feel a lot better now I have been able to make this
decision and my children seem much happier too.*

Example A is all George and how fabulous he is as a Practitioner.
It tells you very little about how George was able to help and
what difference NLP (and George) actually made. It assumes the
reader (i.e. potential client) already knows about NLP and how it
can help, and all it really does is tell us about gorgeous George.

Example B, on the other hand, is far more specific and
focused on the effects of the presenting problem and solution,
rather than on George. It informs the reader (potential client)
how NLP has helped and what a difference it has made. It
provides a story to which someone with a similar fear may
just relate.

So, if you were a member of the public who did want to learn
how to quit smoking, I wonder which story would be more
likely to motivate you into taking some action. And which just
might generate enough interest get into the local paper next
time a journalist is searching for examples of smoking related
success stories. I suspect it would be Example B.

TIP

*Prepare some short promotional success stories/case
studies of your own. Top and tail these when relevant
and use as press releases for local news media.*

Whilst we are quite rightly proud of our achievements and the work we have had to put in to become a top rate NLP Professional, the public don't really know much about the different training organisations or certification bodies. And with all due respect to Richard Bandler and John Grinder, had you actually heard of them *before* you got involved with NLP?

So would you agree it is in all our best interests to promote the practical applications, positive experiences and benefits of NLP to the public first? This way we can start to counter balance the negative press and encourage the public to visit the NLP garden rather than the CBT garden or the hypnotherapy garden. We can then start to ensure NLP is *the* one of the natural solutions chosen by the public when they have a problem.

Changing the public perception of NLP so they find it easier to make this choice

As I mentioned earlier, we are lucky enough to talk to the public on a daily basis, and they are usually those people who have, one way or another, discovered NLP could be the solution to their particular challenge.

So why do they end up contacting us rather than going directly to the practitioner or trainer who will help them with their problem? It seems there are three main reasons, which crop up again and again during these conversations. Generally it seems the public contact us because they are either:

1. *Confused.*

2. *Overwhelmed.*

3. *Seeking reassurance.*

So let's break these down a bit further:

1. Confused. *The public are confused because there is no clear signposting within NLP.*

I spoke to a lovely lady recently who said she had decided to call us 'as a last resort' because she still had no clear idea what would be the best training route for her. She explained she had already spoken to a number of trainers, and said they were all keen to sell their services to her.

But what she actually wanted first was to understand more about NLP per se, why she should consider NLP training, what were the training qualification routes and what could be the consequences in choosing one accrediting body over another. She wanted to understand this before she could start to make a decision about which specific trainer to choose.

Another person I spoke to recently was confused about the acronyms and what they actually meant. Would it be better for him to choose INLPTA, ABNLP or an SNLP approved trainer and which one, if any, was the real governing body for NLP?

NLP is full of jargon and acronyms. NLP may have a great meaning for us, but in reality, what does 'Neuro Linguistic Programming' really mean to the man (or woman) on the street?

I never really appreciated how challenging acronyms and jargon could be to other people until I became a school governor. Here I was, an educated and intelligent adult, moving into the world of education, which is absolutely full of acronyms. I must have sat in the first two or three meetings completely oblivious to what was actually being said, because I was so busy making notes of all the acronyms I needed to Google later.

Let's be honest here for a moment – as a community we understand our own history and on occasions seem to be happy to model our founders and create division within our community. In the past, we have created divisions between the 7 day and 20 day practitioners; or those who have trained through INLPTA, The Professional Guild, SNLP, ABNLP, ITA...it's confusing for anyone on the outside of our community looking in, because they don't know where to start.

Again, if we are being really honest for a moment – as a community, we cannot even agree on a universal definition of NLP, or even one which is widely accepted in the UK. We recently published a Rapport article about the definition of NLP and managed to gather over 30 definitions within two days – all valid and clearly stated...and different.

> **TIP**
>
> **Create a clear definition of NLP to put on your own website . . . and make sure it is one which is understood by the general public. For some examples, see http://www.anlp.org/what-is-nlp.**

So, if we have this much difficulty tying down a definition of NLP, think how confusing it must be for the general public to work out what NLP could do for them. NLP can be so hard to define in simple terms, maybe it would be more useful to use examples rather than definitions.

And whilst we do have a clearly defined training structure for NLP (i.e. Practitioner, Master Practitioner, Trainer) there is no clarity before or after that – we have been asked if an NLP Diploma is the lowest or highest qualification in NLP. We have only recently opened the Pandora's box about Trainers' Training and published a collaboratively produced listing of UK recognised Master Trainers.

So need I go on?

If we, as a community have a bit of confusion around defining NLP, clarifying the qualification structure and where to create a focal point for NLP, it's not surprising the public, looking into our garden for the first time, could be equally confused.

2. Overwhelmed. *The public are overwhelmed because there is so much choice.*

To go back to our garden analogy, at the moment we have every single flower, vegetable and piece of hard landscaping in our garden, which is superb, especially for an options person like me. But this choice can be completely overwhelming for someone coming into the garden for the first time, who is not a gardening expert and who cannot tell the difference between a Quercus *and a* Daucus carota *(an oak tree and a carrot).*

And it's even more confusing because all these plants are everywhere in the garden...carrots sit alongside roses and blackberries grow on top of these, because they are all vying for attention.

Everyone in the garden wants to be noticed, this is understandable...and in our eagerness to be noticed, perhaps we forget there are lots of other gardens for people to choose from, so we could end up putting people off the NLP garden altogether, especially if they are not yet convinced NLP is the right garden to be in.

NLP does not yet have the same universal understanding as, say supermarkets. Everyone, yes everyone, knows the benefits of supermarket shopping, so the supermarkets can afford to vie for our attention by directly criticising their competition (our baked beans are cheaper than Tesco).

The same cannot be said for NLP yet, so there is everything to gain by working together to develop the big picture plan for promoting NLP to the public and getting people into our garden (or supermarket) first.

3. Seeking reassurance. *The public want to know the NLP garden is a safe garden to enter.*

NLP like coaching and many other personal development methodologies is currently unregulated so increasingly the public are looking for reassurance from somewhere, if they choose to come into the NLP garden, they will be protected. Not only are we in an increasingly litigious society, we are also coming out of a recession – emotions are high and funds are low for a lot of your potential clients.

People want to believe their investment in your services will have a positive effect on their lives. It can be a huge investment for them, both in terms of time and financial commitment, so they do want to believe it will work.

Obviously, as a subjective experience, a lot does depend on their attitude and whether or not they are ready to make the necessary changes. But for them to make this choice in the first place, it does help if they have heard or read something positive about NLP.

NLP training and NLP consultations are quite an investment of someone's hard earned money, and they do want guarantees it is going to be money well spent.

I took a call from a psychotherapist who was interested in adding NLP to her portfolio. She specifically wanted an NLP trainer who was accredited by both ABNLP and ANLP and who worked in London. When I suggested the two members who fitted this specific bill, she said she had already looked at them, but their prices were quite high. I did point out the reason for this could possibly be because they were double accredited and were therefore offering the reassurance she was after.

TIP

Collect your own social proof to give your potential clients the reassurance they seek.

So if we were to work together to address these concerns of confusion, overwhelm and reassurance, we could start changing the public perception of NLP so they find it easier to choose NLP.

Appreciating the importance of reputation

The other thing which needs to be addressed when considering raising the profile of NLP is the importance of reputation.

Leaping off a tower in front of my children probably increased their respect for me and my reputation with them, albeit temporarily. Integrity and trust are an important part of the relationship you build with your clients, and they also contribute to your reputation. I am sure you, like me, prefer to purchase goods and services which have either been recommended, or come from a reputable source.

A great example of using reputation to successfully build a business is eBay. eBay is successful as an online marketplace where complete strangers are happy to buy and sell goods to each other online, partly because the participants are fiercely protective of their reputation, which is promoted in the form of feedback. It is vital to have great feedback on eBay so people trust you enough to buy from you. This feedback is measurable and becomes the focus for encouraging positive decisions.

I purchased a great set of bedroom furniture recently, and the lady I bought it from was one of the sweetest people I had ever met. She was so concerned about maintaining her 100% feedback she knocked a bit more money off when I went to collect the items, because she had found a mark earlier which she hadn't mentioned on the listing. So the eBay measure of integrity and trust does seem to work most of the time.

Reputation takes time to build up, and can be destroyed in moments. Just look at the scandal which has haunted MPs since their expenses debacle was exposed. I am sure some MPs were totally honest with their expenses and did only claim what was reasonable and necessary for the performance of their duties. But the reputation of the MPs as a whole was tarnished as a result of those who acted with less integrity than we expected, and abused the trust which we, as a nation of voters, had given them. Perhaps we could introduce eBay style feedback ratings for our MPs.

TIP

Use social media (LinkedIn, Facebook, Twitter to start building your online presence and reputation – use Klout (www.klout.com) to measure your social reach and influence.

When we are able to raise people's awareness of NLP and improve its credibility, then we will all be in a much better position to benefit from the increased demand for the services of NLP Professionals.

There are real benefits to creating positive PR around NLP as a viable solution and therefore raising the profile of NLP as a Profession.

There is a saying 'any publicity is good publicity', and perhaps this depends more on your motives and outcome for generating the publicity in the first place. There are certain 'celebrities' who do seem to believe this, and we are just as likely to read about something terrible they have done as we are to read about their latest success.

Is it possible to measure the impact of PR? It probably depends on the intended outcome. Whilst a newsworthy story raises your profile, I would suggest a positive one increases your business.

Remember the Tiger Woods scandal which hit the headlines following his late night car accident? As a result of this 'less than favourable' exposure, he lost a lot of his sponsorship/advertising deals because the sponsors had no wish to be linked with someone whose reputation had been tarnished.

There are many other celebrities who spring to mind who may have succeeded in getting their picture onto the front page of the national press due to some scandal, but at what cost in terms of finance and reputation?

Hypnotherapy and NLP had their reputation knocked recently when it was publicised, in a national paper and on TV, a cat had successfully joined some of the hypnotherapy and NLP associations. This would not have done a great deal for the reputation of the organisations concerned, and neither did it do much for the reputations of hypnotherapy and NLP.

On the other hand, NLP practitioner, Martin Weaver, had Jaci Stephens, one of the *Daily Mail* journalists as his client, and following her successful sessions, she wrote a very favourable piece about NLP, which featured in the *Daily Mail*. Not only did Martin find himself with a fully booked appointments diary for months afterwards, but also our many other NLP practitioners did too, especially our members, because they benefitted from the knock on effects of Martin's positive publicity.

The more positive news people can read about NLP, the more it does become a credible option for them. Even if, at the time they read about it, they don't have any specific reason for wanting to engage the services of an NLP practitioner, the information may filter into their subconscious and stay there, ready to be recalled at a later date when it is needed.

Publicity, good and bad, ripples outwards, just like the drops of rain landing on a still pond. We know how the communication model works, so it is in our interests to ensure the NLP related messages stored away for future reference are positive ones. This way NLP becomes one of the credible options which is considered when the time is right.

TIP

We all know about cause and effect, and how it can be much more useful for us to be 'at cause'. So take 100% responsibility for building a good reputation for NLP.

To ensure NLP continues to improve its reputation, then we could start to consider the impact of the messages we send out. We know about the communication model and the way we filter and store information in our unconscious mind.

One person who probably does understand the full implication of the communication model and maintaining a good reputation is Gerald Ratner. It was 1991 when he made his now infamous speech to the Institute of Directors, and called his own products, from Ratners the jewellers, 'crap'. This was a joke he had made many times before, but on this occasion, it was reported by the *Daily Mirror*, who implied he was making fun of his own customers.

As a result of this speech, Ratners' shares plummeted, the business suffered and Gerald Ratner lost his job as Chief Executive and Chairman of the world's biggest jewellery company. One word became very costly for the man who had once enjoyed a six figure salary and chauffeur driven limousines.

The world has changed considerably since 1991, and the internet has made everything more accessible to everyone. Gerald Ratner may not have needed to make a grand speech in front of the Institute of Directors today – he could have simply written his observations in his online blog. And we could have found ourselves discussing the implications and effect of his remarks on one of the many online forums. The result, however, for Gerald Ratner could well have been the same and he may not have even needed the publicity of the *Daily Mirror* to expose him has they did.

It seems today everyone has an online presence and raises their profile with social media marketing. We tweet and blog and post our comments on Facebook and LinkedIn, and probably on many other easily accessible online media platforms.

The whole world can, if they choose, read our comments and views about NLP and find out about our heated debates and disagreements and distasteful and personal comments about other NLP practitioners, which sometimes seem to be deliberately designed to shock and fire up debate.

We have dealt with complaints made by members of the public, who are aghast when the details of their private lives or their particular issue have been openly debated, ridiculed and commented upon within an online forum...sometimes without even changing the name of the client.

So we don't necessarily need the *Daily Mirror* to expose these things nowadays because if we choose to write detrimental comments about NLP or the people within our community, they are there, on the internet, for all to see...and this can have a knock on effect for the reputation of NLP as a whole.

TIP

Think about who is going to read your comments before you post them on the internet for your potential clients to read.

Summary

When the public become more aware NLP is a solution to their problem, then they will start to appreciate you could be the NLP Professional to help them. As awareness increases, so does acceptance, and as NLP becomes more widely accepted, there will be increased demands for your services as an NLP Professional.

Raise awareness of NLP

CHAPTER EIGHT

Shaping Your Future in NLP

*'The best teamwork comes from men who
are working independently toward
one goal in unison.'*

James Cash Penney, business man and entrepreneur (1875–1971)

At the end of the day, I understand you ultimately want your business to be more professional, effective and successful.

You want your investment in your NLP training, continuing professional development and business development to pay off and be worthwhile – you want a return on your investment (ROI).

You want to be recognised as a consummate NLP Professional, defined at the beginning of this book as 'A practitioner of NLP, who is serious about their business and who wants to make a difference by delivering their NLP services in a responsible, congruent and ethical way'.

Apart from the tips scattered throughout this book, I have put together a summary of actions you could choose to take and which would enable you to start creating the right mindset to develop a more professional, effective and successful NLP business.

1. **Adopting a professional attitude**

   Choose one of these areas to work on in the next three months:

   ▼ *Create or review your business plan.*

   ▼ *Allocate some quality time in your diary to work 'on' your business.*

   ▼ *Review your personal appearance as an NLP Professional and choose one aspect to improve.*

   Whichever area you choose, make sure you create at least one SMART goal...and email me when you have completed your goal.

2. **Being congruent with what you do**

   ▼ *Choose any NLP strategy and apply it to your business. You have plenty to choose from including well formed outcomes, the presuppositions of NLP, perceptual positions, pacing and leading, cause and effect.*

   ▼ *Re-elicit your business values and prioritise them – check these against both your personal values and your business plan and make sure all aspects align.*

3. **Demonstrating best practice**

   ▼ *If you haven't already got them, create one to one coaching agreements for your clients – these will protect both you and them in the event of any misunderstanding.*

   ▼ *Commit to at least one continual professional development (CPD) activity in the next three months. This can be anything from attending a practice group meeting, reading a relevant book or booking a business workshop/teleseminar.*

4. Appreciating the value of social proof

▼ *Collect testimonials from your next three clients and use them on your website and in your promotional materials (NB. make sure they comply with CAP guidelines).*

▼ *Join a Professional Body or Trade Association. It would be great if this was ANLP...and any professional membership will add to your social proof.*

5. Celebrating our differences

Identify your niche market, by asking yourself the following questions:

▼ *What is your potential niche?*

▼ *What problems could your potential niche possibly solve?*

▼ *Why do these problems continue?*

▼ *Who do you most enjoy working with?*

6. Working collaboratively

Make contact with and introduce yourself to at least one helping professional in your local area. Just be curious and explore potential avenues for working collaboratively.

7. Raising awareness of NLP

Write at least one success story which is relevant to your niche and use this to promote your services and obtain some extra PR via local media (for example, newspapers, local magazines and local radio).

Final thoughts...

It is easier than we realise, sometimes, to be the difference that makes a difference, and we all do make a difference to someone, every day...remember, you cannot not communicate, and communicating does have an effect on others.

The smallest actions can sometimes have a knock on effect and make a difference to the lives of others. You only have to think about the ripples which radiate across a pond when you throw one pebble into its centre. Every one of us is one of those pebbles, and our pond is everywhere – our home, our place of work, the supermarket, the cinema, the restaurant, or even the car park.

Once we have learned about NLP, we do use elements with varying degrees of unconscious competence. Sometimes, it is just our acceptance of the presuppositions of NLP which enables us to view things slightly differently and to take a more philosophical viewpoint.

Sometimes it is our understanding of the communication model, or our ability to naturally step into another person's shoes and see the world from their perspective. Whatever it is, our understanding does mean we are able to approach many situations in a different and more useful way. However we choose to apply our understanding of NLP, it does have an impact on our lives and the lives of others.

Think about the knock on effect and greater social impact you could be having, every day as you use your NLP to enrich the lives of others.

It follows if this knock on effect can happen so easily, then we can also have unknown positive effects on others. Alan Briscoe is a Trainer with Mind Cymru's Positive Choices Project and he runs a two day workshop called ASIST (Applied Suicide Intervention Skills Training). They provide practical training for caregivers seeking to prevent the immediate risk of suicide, because, so often in these situations, there is a reluctance to get involved for fear of making things worse, not knowing what to do, or just by assuming it is someone else's responsibility.

Alan received this feedback from someone who had completed his workshop:

I wanted to let you know how much your training helped me today. I was on the train home from visiting my mother when I saw that the lady sitting opposite me was crying. Normally I wouldn't have said anything, scared that someone would think I was interfering, but as I sat there I kept remembering how on the ASIST course we had learned about how important it is to follow your gut instinct – I mean, she just looked so upset. So I started talking to her, and she didn't resent it at all, but seemed relieved to be able to talk to someone.

When I asked her if she was thinking of killing herself, she just sat there nodding, for what seemed like ages and then looked at me and said thank you. In the past I would have been terrified of saying the wrong thing, but today I just followed what you showed us in the training. I felt really calm and focused on her.

We carried on talking – of course, I missed my stop, but she really needed someone and today that was me. It has made me realise how locked away in our own lives we can be, but how amazing it is to be there for someone else, even a complete stranger. Anyway thank you again, the training was absolutely fabulous, best course I've ever been on – and today I might have just saved a life.

So, whether we know it or not, we are making a difference.

Go back to the secret NLP garden for a moment, and consider your own place within it. It doesn't matter if you choose to be a strawberry plant, a daffodil, or an oak tree. You can be the rope holding the garden swing, the cherub in the water fountain, or one of the succulent young carrots in the nursery bed.

It's a large garden, and whatever you choose to be within this garden, there is a place for you. And the thing which makes this garden so appealing is its diversity – there is something in it to appeal to everyone, even those who just want to come and sit for a while, and enjoy everything there is on offer.

The secret which makes this garden work so well is the way every element has its own identity, and yet works together and complements the other elements. Despite there being a great deal of diversity within it, there is a place for everything and everything has a place – and because of this, it means anyone coming into the garden can find what they are looking for, quickly and easily and start to enjoy what the NLP garden can offer them.

Remember the Decision Tree for a moment... this is where we can work together to make a difference in society – at the level where the public have a problem and want some options for helping them solve their problem.

You may think I am painting a rosy picture (no pun intended) and this view is too idealistic. We can continue to promote every flower, vegetable and feature as an individual unique aspect of a garden... and yet not so many people notice one daffodil, however stunning it is.

Sometimes, to be noticed and make sure our beacon is shining brightly, we have to work together to make this bold and collective statement first – and the great thing about coalition is it is about working together whilst maintaining our own identity.

I think sometimes, it is forgotten the thing we all have in common is we all embrace and believe in NLP. It is NLP which hold us all together as a community, and gives us our place in this particular secret garden.

You could argue it is solely the responsibility of organisations like ANLP to increase that public awareness and make sure that more of the public do know about NLP. And I would agree with you ANLP does have a responsibility to inform and educate the public about NLP. ANLP also has a role in informing the public about all the benefits of NLP and the practical ways in which NLP can be used…and there are many.

And yet we can only do this with your help, because at the end of the day, we are promoting *your* services to the public, not ours.

It is my dream to get NLP recognised by the education system, partly because of this knock on effect. Imagine the rippling social impact which could be made to primary school children when their teachers have a working knowledge and understanding of NLP. Imagine the difference which could be made to secondary school students when they experience some of the positive impact of NLP for themselves. Imagine how this could help with their confidence levels at exam time or during interviews, for starters.

Imagine the knock on effect of this social impact on society in a few years time, when every person leaving school has heard of and experienced NLP. This would mean an understanding of NLP would go with these students into their careers, wherever this may be…and so then, when these organisations are approached by an NLP practitioner in the future, there will already be someone within who can support the value of your work based on their own experience at school.

By adopting the principles laid out in this book, we can all play a part in ensuring there is a successful, professional, responsible element within the field of NLP. At the moment, we have the opportunity to shape the future for our profession and decide on the course we want NLP to take in the future – the power lies with us, as NLP Professionals to make this happen.

The Presuppositions of NLP[1]

The principles which form the foundation of NLP have been modelled from key people who consistently produced superb results, as well as from systems theory and natural laws.

As well as a set of powerful skills, NLP is a philosophy and an attitude that is useful when your goal is excellence in whatever you do. We invite you to discover what happens in your life if you simply act 'as if' the following statements are true...

Have respect for the other person's model of the world.

We are all unique and experience the world in different ways. Everyone is individual and has their own special way of being.

The map is not the territory.

People respond to their map of reality, not to reality itself. How people make sense of the world around them is through their senses and from their own personal experience; this means that each individual's perception of an event is different.

Mind and body form a linked system.

Your mental attitude affects your body and your health and, in turn, how you behave.

If what you are doing isn't working, do something else.

Flexibility is the key to success.

Choice is better than no choice.

Having options can provide more opportunities for achieving results.

We are always communicating.

Even when we remain silent, we are communicating. Non-verbal communication can account for a large proportion of a message.

The meaning of your communication is the response you get.

While your intention may be clear to you, it is the other person's interpretation and response that reflects your effectiveness. NLP teaches you the skills and flexibility to ensure that the message you send equals the message they receive.

There is no failure, only feedback.

What seemed like failure can be thought of as success that just stopped too soon. With this understanding, we can stop blaming ourselves and others, find solutions and improve the quality of what we do.

Behind every behaviour there is a positive intention.

When we understand that other people have some positive intention in what they say and do (however annoying and negative it may seem to us), it can be easier to stop getting angry and start to move forward.

Anything can be accomplished if the task is broken down into small enough steps.

Achievement becomes easier if activities are manageable; NLP can help you learn how to analyse what needs to be done and find ways to be both efficient and effective.

Create a More Professional, Effective and Successful **NLP** Business

Endorsements

Do you want to create a Professional NLP Business? What would that require? Look no further than this succinct book, *The NLP Professional*. Here, Karen Moxom, the Managing Director of ANLP, has answered these questions and identified the strategy you will need, here you will find both the requisite skills and attitude.

L. Michael Hall, PhD, Neuro-Semantics Executive Director

Karen has already probably done more than most people to promote high ethical standards and professionalism amongst practitioners of NLP. This book is another manifestation of that commitment. It's one thing to talk about integrity and authenticity, and quite another to model and communicate them in such a down-to-earth way.

Fortunately, it is very evident this book is based not just on Karen's passionate beliefs about how to create a better world, but also on her ability to practise what she preaches; it is encouraging to know that the person who speaks to you here from the printed page is so congruent with the professional code she describes.

Paul Tosey, PhD, Senior Lecturer, University of Surrey

When I am asked to review or offer an opinion on a new NLP book, I usually politely pass on the opportunity and inwardly groan! This is because many NLP books are in my opinion mostly the exact same ideas and concepts recycled! I am however delighted to report that *The NLP Professional* is very different. It's full of useful, practical advice that anyone in the field would do well to read. It's wonderfully jargon free and full of the author's personal experience and observations which make it a good read for both those already in the field and also those who have an interest but have not yet explored the world of NLP. The author's comments on the misuse of language and typical abbreviations in NLP are most welcome as this is in my experience a major source of confusion for the public.

Nick Kemp, Author, Trainer, Therapist

The NLP Professional is an accessible and compelling read, containing a wealth of information and experience of enormous potential value to NLP professionals. From newly qualified practitioners, to seasoned experts and trainers who might wish to reflect again on how they are being perceived (and offering insight to those they train on how to get started ethically in an NLP business) – this is a must read.

Karen shares from her extensive knowledge on NLP issues, giving an insight into how the world perceives NLP in practice. This gives a unique opportunity for others to model real professional integrity and passion and to stand on the shoulders of a true giant in the field, someone who is working passionately and selflessly to develop, build and enhance NLP, its reputation and professional standards in this new, exciting, constantly evolving and emerging profession.

Dr Suzanne Henwood, Associate Professor,
Faculty of Social and Health Sciences, Unitec, Auckland

There are hundreds of books on NLP to choose from but this is the *first* written to support NLP professionals and it is badly needed. Karen Moxom takes you through the vital topics of working using NLP, from personal attitude and professionalism to marketing, collaboration and raising awareness. She achieves it in an easy to read style with copious personal stories and references to illustrate her points. The book is also a cry from the heart of one who leads the top UK NLP body, the Association for NLP (ANLP), to us professionals – to pool resources, celebrate differences and work together to spread news of the extraordinary and powerful science of NLP for the good of every community. Full of important professional tips, useful references and good sense – a book definitely not to miss if you are using NLP for your work.

Judy Apps, Coach, NLP Trainer,
Speaker and Author of *Voice of Influence*

At last! Thanks to Karen there is now a book which will allow everyone to understand the benefits of NLP, how they can reach their full potential and ensure they are set up for success in the future. Karen's knowledge, passion and expertise shine through every single page and this is a book that will make you think and think again.

Emma Wimhurst, Business Mentor,
Author and Motivational Business Speaker

This book provides a great foundation for NLP Professionals. It is particularly valuable to new NLP Practitioners and Trainers looking to set up a business. I really like the emphasis on the importance of ethics and supervision referred to throughout. I will recommend this book to all our students past, present and future.

Melody Cheal, MSc Applied Positive Psychology,
Master Trainer of NLP and Co-developer of PSiNLP

This is a professional, honest and brave publication by Karen. This book provides an excellent guide on the 'how to' of transferring your learning NLP into a successful business venture. Readers are invited to think holistically about their NLP career from multiple perspectives.

Karen seamlessly integrates the entire attitude of NLP, the presuppositions and philosophical framework modelled from Erickson, Satir and Perls with a comprehensive understanding and explanation of key business processes. Any reader will gain great value from the many tips and advisory suggestions that are offered.

I am delighted to endorse it.

Lisa Wake, MSc, RGN,
Director Awaken Consulting & Training Services Ltd

The NLP Professional is a unique book from a unique person who is uniquely placed within the NLP world. Because of her inclusive nature, Karen Moxom has one of the most balanced and objective views of the current NLP Community. In this book, she integrates this refreshingly objective stance with a delightfully personal touch. *The NLP Professional* is written from the heart of a mind with integrity and intelligence and you will find it well worth your attention.

Joe Cheal, NLP Master Trainer, Editor of *Acuity: The ANLP Journal,*
Partner in The GWiz Learning Partnership

Marketing yourself as an NLP professional is a minefield, and this book is a handy map. It's so much more than a campaign manifesto for the professionalisation of NLP. In its clear and simple text, you'll discover the principles, the people, and a host of practical tips to help you build a solid reputation and a commercial future, both for yourself and for your NLP colleagues.

Judy Rees, Co-Author of *Clean Language:*
Revealing Metaphors and Opening Minds

This book is a delight to consume in depth when first starting your NLP business and for seasoned NLPers to use as a reference guide and keep on the bookshelf. As well as being an easy and entertaining read, it is full of tips and references, all of which will guide your business planning and development process. It provides a framework for 'being' a professional and highlights the pitfalls that many NLPers have fallen into, while gently challenging those who have not yet been as congruent and ethical as the profession deserves.

Karen modestly shares her own journey into the NLP world. Her unique experience of 'having lived the profession from a meta position' enables her to provide expert guidance on how to 'get it right' from the beginning in a style which is full of common sense, integrity and fun!

Sally Vanson, Director of post-graduate NLP and Coaching programmes; The Performance Solution

The NLP Professional is essential reading for 'NLPers' serious about using their skills to make a difference. It contains comforting confirmation that the 'good' things we are doing, are well worth the investment and the time for us as individuals, and also for the benefit of the wider NLP community. It also serves as a reminder that there are always areas in which we can improve our businesses and why perhaps it is so important we begin to take those next steps.

Karen is exceptionally well placed from both a personal and business point of view to highlight these guiding principles. She is an award winning business woman with a passion to bring even more credibility to NLP. In her role as the leader of the ANLP she has over the years listened to the views of thousands of people including members of the public, NLP practitioners and trainers.

This book pulls together best practice across many fields and applies them to NLP. Karen gives easy to understand illustrations of the key points by bringing in examples from her work and home life making it an informative, personable and easy read. Highly recommended.

Dee Clayton, NLP Trainer and Director
Simply Amazing Training Ltd

The NLP Professional is a really useful guide for all NLPers, whether they want to create a successful NLP business or simply to use NLP in a professional manner. The book is full of tips and ideas to take on board, particularly in the early stages of running an NLP-based business. It also raises some essential issues around the development and professionalisation of the whole NLP field, and refers to important prevailing legislation which impacts on everyone running an NLP business.

Mirroring Karen's natural approachable and personable manner, *The NLP Professional* is written in conversational style, full of stories and anecdotes. Regardless of the extent to which you adopt Karen's tips, considering them will help you to clarify and achieve your business and professional goals.

Jeremy Lazarus, Master Trainer of NLP,
Director, The Lazarus Consultancy Ltd

In this deceptively simple book Karen has laid out nothing less than a manifesto to take NLP through the 21st century and beyond.

Taking a no-nonsense approach she rightly chides and challenges a number of negative strategies that some in the NLP world express. However, like a farmer who knows that seeds can both grow into a crop as well as be feed for much needed wildlife, she scatters a liberal amount of practical and positive advice. She directs us to real actions, based on her own success and proven business practice that we can all benefit from applying.

If your need is to find a treasure trove of practical ways to improve your practice of NLP to yourself and your clients then *The NLP Professional* is it. If you are starting out then it lays down some really useful pathways that will accelerate your success and if you are more experienced then it's a superb quality check list against which to model yourself.

The NLP Professional is NLP modelling at its best, in that if we don't present our values and our ethics freely and openly in the world, and so provide that model, then against what do we measure ourselves? Karen presents a positive and achievable archetype of real world applications of NLP.

Martin Weaver, NLP Psychotherapist, Supervisor and Trainer

Whether you want to use NLP purely for personal development or become a user of NLP to enhance your qualified area of expertise, Karen Moxom's book *The NLP Professional* is not only an amazing and well prepared guide, it is also a resource. (I got some tips from it!) Karen has put down in writing many of the statements, I and other NLP Trainers make in respect of what NLP is and how it is put to use ethically, morally and effectively.

Not only does Karen present NLP and how we use it and sometimes some people misuse it (!), Karen calls for uniform standards and working together as an NLP Team. She also presents practical business tips, as well as some wonderful metaphors from the world of gardening to get her message across.

This is a well thought out, well structured book, drawing on her own and others experiences. For me, as an Accredited and Certified Trainer of NLP this is not just a 'recommended read' for those on my past, present and future NLP courses – it is also an 'I really ask you to consider this book and what it says' (for the internally referenced among us).

Rosie O'Hara, Director NLP Highland,
Words that Change Minds LAB Profile Consultant and Trainer
and published author

I'm so glad Karen's brought this book into the world. I'd recommend it not only for NLP Professionals but for anyone with an interest in learning more about NLP, hiring an NLP coach or embarking on some training themselves. It's filled with common sense, good humour and practical advice.

I've been an NLP Master Practitioner for several years but kept pausing my reading to reflect on my own practice as *The NLP Professional* prompted ideas about things I can do differently. It also inspired some changes to my website (which now seem so obvious!). An enjoyable and practical read which could help all of us NLP Professionals pull together as ambassadors for NLP as well as getting more from our private practices. Loved it.

Eve Menezes Cunningham, Freelance Writer / Journalist specialising in psychology, health and wellbeing

Karen's book sets the benchmarks for effective, ethical and professional NLP practice and business. Bags of user-friendly practical advice, resources and examples, with NLP modelled and woven through every page! A must read both for the newly qualified and established practitioners serious about CPD.

Sharon Eden, MA, Inner Leadership Coach, Psychotherapist, Speaker and Author

In *The NLP Professional*, ANLP's leader Karen Moxom gives freely and generously from her own insights, lessons and successes as well as drawing on those of others putting NLP to work. The result is a richly illuminating perspective of NLP today which is wider than most of us can see.

In her friendly style, Karen starts from the first principles of business and professionalism and moves to her inspired vision for a collaborative future, along the way showing how to embed NLP into good business practice. She provides both guidance which is especially valuable for those new to this work, and well-founded orientation which is enlightening for everyone in this complex, wonderfully rewarding field.

Faith Tait, Co-Creator, Integral NLP+. Trainer, Coach, Speaker, Writer

The NLP Professional is an encouraging and timely guide to promoting professional integrity, high standards and credibility in our unregulated and increasingly diverse field.

I agree wholeheartedly with the strong recommendation that NLP Practitioners commit to deepening their skills and to being competent, congruent and ethical in their practice.

Skill-based, systemic NLP is already making a significant and unique, positive contribution to many individuals and communities and in our wider, changing world.

Karen Moxom demonstrates with a lively mix of personal stories, metaphors, business tips and all-round useful advice that she is a generous, passionate and thoughtful champion of this vision.

Judith Lowe, PPD Learning Ltd, NLP Training Institute, London

The NLP Professional confirms Karen Moxom as the leading advocate for a Professional approach to NLP. This book succinctly highlights the importance of the NLP Professional to create a more successful NLP business and in turn contribute to the universal recognition of NLP.

Beejal Shah, Senior Lecturer and Coach, University of Hertfordshire

When NLP students complete their training, we are asked many questions about setting up in practice, from professional memberships through to ethics and the scope of their work based on their NLP training. In the past, we have answered these questions as best as we can, or pointed them in the right direction for the information.

From this point forward, *The NLP Professional* is the resource we will be recommending. It is full of helpful guidance, suggestions and convincing strategies for new practitioners to set up a successful and professional practice.

However, this book is more than a success guide for new NLP practitioners. It's a revolutionary call to NLP Training Institutes. It challenges us to walk the talk and embrace key professional attitudes.

We must rise to the challenge set out in this book or we will miss out on the opportunity to put NLP Training and practice on to a professional level, where we know it belongs.

Tony Nutley, Director and Trainer at UKCPD

This thought provoking, practical and inspiring book is a wonderful guide that will empower NLP professionals to either start or further develop their NLP business. It highlights important aspects such as procedures, processes, niche markets, operating within our 'scope of practice', legislation and standards; making complex issues accessible and easy to understand with website addresses for further clarification.

I believe if you get one good thing from a book it's worthwhile, and this book will give you many. Through the very nature of modelling, NLP enables us to stand on the shoulders of giants. Now you can stand on Karen's shoulders; Hertfordshire Woman of the Year in 2009 – who better to help you be the best NLP Professional you can be. The choice is yours!

Julie Inglis, NLP Trainer and Creator
of Ripple of Change ® methodologies

On reflection this book does exactly what I would of expected – if you have experienced Karen Moxom for real then you will know what I mean.

Clear writing, structure and the attention to the 'ordinary' makes this publication a must for all grass root practitioners, trainers and others interested in NLP.

Karen's blend of energy and commitment are apparent throughout.

Brian Morton, NLP Trainer

An excellent introduction for those wishing to start up an NLP business. A clear, thoughtful structure takes both novices and experienced practitioners through practical issues on how to create a credible business in the field of NLP. Liberally sprinkled with stories and case studies which illustrate the concepts nicely and keeps jargon to the minimum. The whole book makes setting up a credible NLP business reasonable, achievable and commonsense.

Jane Douglas, NLP Trainer

Karen's passion for NLP and business is now encapsulated brilliantly in her book for us all to benefit from. Many people struggle with congruence and confidence in building their business. Karen's book will be a very useful tool to help drive success.

Bev James, CEO The Academy Group and Author of *Do it! Or Ditch it – 8 steps from the millionaires' mentor – turn ideas into action and make decisions that count*

About the Author

Karen Moxom is the Managing Director of the Association for NLP, an independent award winning social enterprise specialising in membership services for NLP Professionals. She is motivated to do the best she can to help NLP become more credible, so it will be embraced by the education system and will positively influence more young people, like her own two sons, to achieve their full potential.

As well as running ANLP, Karen is the editor of *Rapport*, the magazine for NLP Professionals, and the publisher of *Acuity* and the NLP Research Journal, *Current Research in NLP.*

Before taking over the reins at ANLP, Karen was a management accountant and trainer, and ran her own company which focussed on facilitating small businesses to manage their finances more effectively.

Until recently she was Chair of Governors at her son's school, she is a Scout helper and she is part of the Developing Special Provision Locally Parent Reference group for Hertfordshire

County Council. She was awarded Hertfordshire Woman of the Year in the 2009 Hertfordshire Business Awards.

She is a single mum, and lives in Hertfordshire with her sons and their two cats.

Karen can be contacted by email at **vision@anlp.org.** You will find Karen on Linked In and Twitter, and you can follow her personal blog on **www.karenmoxom.com**

Notes

Notes

Notes

Notes